A true and almost incredible report of an Englishman, that (being cast away in the good ship called the Assension in Cambaya, the farthest part of the East Indies) trauelled by land thorow many vnknowne kingdomes and great cities (1631)

Robert Coverte

A true and almost incredible report of an Englishman, that (being cast away in the good ship called the Assension in Cambaya, the farthest part of the East Indies) trauelled by land thorow many vnknowne kingdomes and great cities

Coverte, Robert.
Printer's name from STC.
With a final colophon leaf.
The first leaf and the last leaf are blank.
Running title reads: The voyage and trauels of Robert Couert.
[8], 68, [4] p.
London : Printed by I[ohn] N[orton] for Hugh Perry, and are to bee sold at his shop, at the signe of the Harrow in Brittaines-Burse, 1631.
STC (2nd ed.) / 5897
English
Reproduction of the original in the Henry E. Huntington Library and Art Gallery

Early English Books Online (EEBO) Editions

Imagine holding history in your hands.

Now you can. Digitally preserved and previously accessible only through libraries as Early English Books Online, this rare material is now available in single print editions. Thousands of books written between 1475 and 1700 and ranging from religion to astronomy, medicine to music, can be delivered to your doorstep in individual volumes of high-quality historical reproductions.

We have been compiling these historic treasures for more than 70 years. Long before such a thing as "digital" even existed, ProQuest founder Eugene Power began the noble task of preserving the British Museum's collection on microfilm. He then sought out other rare and endangered titles, providing unparalleled access to these works and collaborating with the world's top academic institutions to make them widely available for the first time. This project furthers that original vision.

These texts have now made the full journey -- from their original printing-press versions available only in rare-book rooms to online library access to new single volumes made possible by the partnership between artifact preservation and modern printing technology. A portion of the proceeds from every book sold supports the libraries and institutions that made this collection possible, and that still work to preserve these invaluable treasures passed down through time.

This is history, traveling through time since the dawn of printing to your own personal library.

Initial Proquest EEBO Print Editions collections include:

Early Literature

This comprehensive collection begins with the famous Elizabethan Era that saw such literary giants as Chaucer, Shakespeare and Marlowe, as well as the introduction of the sonnet. Traveling through Jacobean and Restoration literature, the highlight of this series is the Pollard and Redgrave 1475-1640 selection of the rarest works from the English Renaissance.

Early Documents of World History

This collection combines early English perspectives on world history with documentation of Parliament records, royal decrees and military documents that reveal the delicate balance of Church and State in early English government. For social historians, almanacs and calendars offer insight into daily life of common citizens. This exhaustively complete series presents a thorough picture of history through the English Civil War.

Historical Almanacs

Historically, almanacs served a variety of purposes from the more practical, such as planting and harvesting crops and plotting nautical routes, to predicting the future through the movements of the stars. This collection provides a wide range of consecutive years of "almanacks" and calendars that depict a vast array of everyday life as it was several hundred years ago.

Early History of Astronomy & Space

Humankind has studied the skies for centuries, seeking to find our place in the universe. Some of the most important discoveries in the field of astronomy were made in these texts recorded by ancient stargazers, but almost as impactful were the perspectives of those who considered their discoveries to be heresy. Any independent astronomer will find this an invaluable collection of titles arguing the truth of the cosmic system.

Early History of Industry & Science

Acting as a kind of historical Wall Street, this collection of industry manuals and records explores the thriving industries of construction; textile, especially wool and linen; salt; livestock; and many more.

Early English Wit, Poetry & Satire

The power of literary device was never more in its prime than during this period of history, where a wide array of political and religious satire mocked the status quo and poetry called humankind to transcend the rigors of daily life through love, God or principle. This series comments on historical patterns of the human condition that are still visible today.

Early English Drama & Theatre

This collection needs no introduction, combining the works of some of the greatest canonical writers of all time, including many plays composed for royalty such as Queen Elizabeth I and King Edward VI. In addition, this series includes history and criticism of drama, as well as examinations of technique.

Early History of Travel & Geography

Offering a fascinating view into the perception of the world during the sixteenth and seventeenth centuries, this collection includes accounts of Columbus's discovery of the Americas and encompasses most of the Age of Discovery, during which Europeans and their descendants intensively explored and mapped the world. This series is a wealth of information from some the most groundbreaking explorers.

Early Fables & Fairy Tales

This series includes many translations, some illustrated, of some of the most well-known mythologies of today, including Aesop's Fables and English fairy tales, as well as many Greek, Latin and even Oriental parables and criticism and interpretation on the subject.

Early Documents of Language & Linguistics

The evolution of English and foreign languages is documented in these original texts studying and recording early philology from the study of a variety of languages including Greek, Latin and Chinese, as well as multilingual volumes, to current slang and obscure words. Translations from Latin, Hebrew and Aramaic, grammar treatises and even dictionaries and guides to translation make this collection rich in cultures from around the world.

Early History of the Law

With extensive collections of land tenure and business law "forms" in Great Britain, this is a comprehensive resource for all kinds of early English legal precedents from feudal to constitutional law, Jewish and Jesuit law, laws about public finance to food supply and forestry, and even "immoral conditions." An abundance of law dictionaries, philosophy and history and criticism completes this series.

Early History of Kings, Queens and Royalty

This collection includes debates on the divine right of kings, royal statutes and proclamations, and political ballads and songs as related to a number of English kings and queens, with notable concentrations on foreign rulers King Louis IX and King Louis XIV of France, and King Philip II of Spain. Writings on ancient rulers and royal tradition focus on Scottish and Roman kings, Cleopatra and the Biblical kings Nebuchadnezzar and Solomon.

Early History of Love, Marriage & Sex

Human relationships intrigued and baffled thinkers and writers well before the postmodern age of psychology and self-help. Now readers can access the insights and intricacies of Anglo-Saxon interactions in sex and love, marriage and politics, and the truth that lies somewhere in between action and thought.

Early History of Medicine, Health & Disease

This series includes fascinating studies on the human brain from as early as the 16th century, as well as early studies on the physiological effects of tobacco use. Anatomy texts, medical treatises and wound treatment are also discussed, revealing the exponential development of medical theory and practice over more than two hundred years.

Early History of Logic, Science and Math

The "hard sciences" developed exponentially during the 16th and 17th centuries, both relying upon centuries of tradition and adding to the foundation of modern application, as is evidenced by this extensive collection. This is a rich collection of practical mathematics as applied to business, carpentry and geography as well as explorations of mathematical instruments and arithmetic; logic and logicians such as Aristotle and Socrates; and a number of scientific disciplines from natural history to physics.

Early History of Military, War and Weaponry

Any professional or amateur student of war will thrill at the untold riches in this collection of war theory and practice in the early Western World. The Age of Discovery and Enlightenment was also a time of great political and religious unrest, revealed in accounts of conflicts such as the Wars of the Roses.

Early History of Food

This collection combines the commercial aspects of food handling, preservation and supply to the more specific aspects of canning and preserving, meat carving, brewing beer and even candy-making with fruits and flowers, with a large resource of cookery and recipe books. Not to be forgotten is a "the great eater of Kent," a study in food habits.

Early History of Religion

From the beginning of recorded history we have looked to the heavens for inspiration and guidance. In these early religious documents, sermons, and pamphlets, we see the spiritual impact on the lives of both royalty and the commoner. We also get insights into a clergy that was growing ever more powerful as a political force. This is one of the world's largest collections of religious works of this type, revealing much about our interpretation of the modern church and spirituality.

Early Social Customs

Social customs, human interaction and leisure are the driving force of any culture. These unique and quirky works give us a glimpse of interesting aspects of day-to-day life as it existed in an earlier time. With books on games, sports, traditions, festivals, and hobbies it is one of the most fascinating collections in the series.

The BiblioLife Network

This project was made possible in part by the BiblioLife Network (BLN), a project aimed at addressing some of the huge challenges facing book preservationists around the world. The BLN includes libraries, library networks, archives, subject matter experts, online communities and library service providers. We believe every book ever published should be available as a high-quality print reproduction; printed on-demand anywhere in the world. This insures the ongoing accessibility of the content and helps generate sustainable revenue for the libraries and organizations that work to preserve these important materials.

The following book is in the "public domain" and represents an authentic reproduction of the text as printed by the original publisher. While we have attempted to accurately maintain the integrity of the original work, there are sometimes problems with the original work or the micro-film from which the books were digitized. This can result in minor errors in reproduction. Possible imperfections include missing and blurred pages, poor pictures, markings and other reproduction issues beyond our control. Because this work is culturally important, we have made it available as part of our commitment to protecting, preserving, and promoting the world's literature.

GUIDE TO FOLD-OUTS MAPS and OVERSIZED IMAGES

The book you are reading was digitized from microfilm captured over the past thirty to forty years. Years after the creation of the original microfilm, the book was converted to digital files and made available in an online database.

In an online database, page images do not need to conform to the size restrictions found in a printed book. When converting these images back into a printed bound book, the page sizes are standardized in ways that maintain the detail of the original. For large images, such as fold-out maps, the original page image is split into two or more pages

Guidelines used to determine how to split the page image follows:

- Some images are split vertically; large images require vertical and horizontal splits.
- For horizontal splits, the content is split left to right.
- For vertical splits, the content is split from top to bottom.
- For both vertical and horizontal splits, the image is processed from top left to bottom right.

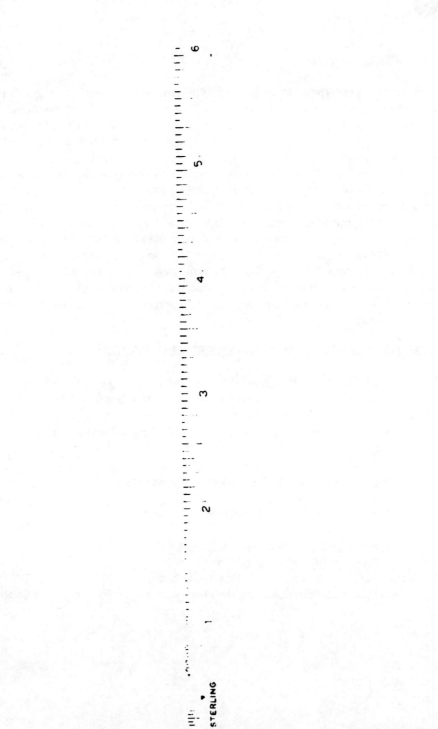

STERLING

A TRVE AND ALMOST INCRE-

dible Report of an Englishman, that
(being cast away in the good Ship called
the *Assension* in *Cambaya*, the farthest part of
the *East Indies*) trauelled by Land thorow
many vnknowne *Kingdomes* and
great Cities.

VVith a particular Description of all
those Kingdomes, Cities, and People:

As also,

A Relation of their commodities and manner of
Traffiqne, and at what seasons of the yeere
they are most in vse. Fayth-
fully related :

WITH A DISCOVERY OF A GREAT
Emperour called the Great *Mogoll*, a Prince,
not till now knowne to our Eng-
lish Nation.

By Captaine *Robert Couert*.

LONDON.

Printed by *I. N.* for *Hugh Perry*, and are to bee
sold at his shop, at the signe of the *Harrow*
in *Brittaines-Burse*. 1631.

TO THE RIGHT
HONOVRABLE, RO-
BERT EARLE OF SALISBVRY,
KNIGHT OF THE MOST HO-
nourable Order of the Garter, Vicount
Cranborne, Lord C E C I L *of Eſſindon*, Lord *high*
Treaſurer of England, Chancellour of the *Vni-*
uerſity of Cambridge, *and one of his Maie-*
ſties moſt Honourable Priuy
Councell.

A S the moſt noble Mæ-
cenas of all good *Arts*,
& the moſt worthy Pa-
tron of all ſuch as can
any way merit of their
Countrey: *I* haue electedyou (Right
Honourable Lord) to whom *I* haue
preſumed) encouraged by your knowne
grace and Clemency) to dedicate theſe

A 4   my

my tedious and dangerous Trauels:
In which, your Honour shall finde vn-
doubtedly all truth, and some nouelty;
if after your more weighty and serious
Considerations, you will daigne the
perusall of this my rude and vnpolisht
discourse. For being shipwrackt in
Cambaya, the farthest part of the
East Indies, and not despairing in the
power of the Almighty, of my safe returne to my Countrey: Leauing the
rest, to the number of 75. that would
not hazard so desperate and vnex-
pected an vndertaking, I aduentured
to passe thorow many vnknown Kingdomes and Cities ouer Land: of all
which, I haue (to my plain vnderstanding) made a particular and faithfull
discouery: Protesting to your Honor, that in all my trauels and (almost
incredible

incredible dangers) *I haue heere ex-*
preft no more then I haue directly seen,
and to my great sufferance and diffi-
cultie prooued. Pardon, I intreat your
Lordship, this my presumption, in se-
lecting you the Noble & worthy Pa-
tron to so rude a discourse, whose sim-
plenesse is onely excused in the Truth.
That granted, I shall thinke my selfe
most comforted after all my precedent
Hazards, that your Honor will but
daigne to accept of this report.

Your Lordships
Humbly denoted,
Robert Coverte.

To the Reader.

Rcceiue, Courteous Reader, a true report of my dangerous Trauels, which will (I make no question) be as pleasing to thee in reading, as they were painefull to mee in suffering. Heere thou mayeft safely and without danger see that, which hath coft mee many a tedious and weary ftep; many a cold and comfortleffe lodging; and many a thin and hungry meale. I publifh not thefe my Aduentures in my pride or arrogancy: But I thinke, I fhould prooue ingratefull to my preferuer, not to let the world know his miraculous power, in safeguarding mee beyond mine owne hope or mans imagination. The report of thefe my perils are freely thine, mine haue onely been the dangers and sufferance. Be thou as well pleased with my faithfull difcouery, as I am contented with my hard and painefull pilgrimage.

Thine,
Robert Covert.

A TRVE AND

almost incredible report of an *Eng-*
lishman, that (being cast away in the ship
called the *Assention* in *Cambaya* the
farthest part of the *East Indies*) trauelled
by Land through many vnknowne
Kingdomes and great
Cities.

He 14. day of March, 1607. wée
came into the Downes, and
there ancozed against Deale, a-
bout 3. miles from Sandwich,
where wée stated vntill the 25.
day of the same moneth, being
by computation the first day of
the yéere, 1608. vpon which day,
about foure of the clocke in the
mozning, wée waighed ancoz and past by Douer, be-
twéene thzée and foure of the clocke in the afternoone,
without any staying, but giuing them notice with 3.
péeces of Ozdnance of ours passing by, and so passed
fozwards some thzée leagues, and then by a contrary
winde wée were dziuen backe againe into Douer rcade,
where wée ancozed and staied till fiue of the clocke in
the mozning, being the twenty first day of March, and
then weighing ancoz, wée sailed some thzée leagues,
when the winde contrarying constrained vs againe to
cast ancoz vntill the 27. day in the mozning about se-

B   uen

nen oz eyght of the clocke, and then hauing a faire gale
of winde, we sailed to Plimouth, where wee arriued the
29. day betwæue tenne and eleuen of the clocke in the
fozenœne, where wœ stayed till the thirty one day of
March. And then hauing a faire gale of winde, wee
waighed ancoz and sailed vntill wee came in sight of
an Jland called the Sauages, on Sunday being the
tenth day of Aprill, being about fiue hundzed leagues
from Plimouth, and still sailed fozwards vntill the
next mozning, that wœ came within sight of the grand
Canaries, which belong to the Spaniard. And vpon
the twelfth day of Aprill, about eight oz nine of the
clocke in the night wœ ancozed, and discharged a péce
of Ozdnance, foz a boate to come abooze, but to no ef-
fect: Foz befoze our arriuall in the roade, there was a
ramoz of twelue saile of Flemmings that were comming
that way, to no good intent (as the Spaniards after-
ward told vs) to bœ some of those Flemmings that had
ouerrunne the rest, whereupon they sent vp into the
Conntrey foz one hundzed and fiftie hozse and foote oz
moze, foz their defence and safeguard (if nœds should
bœe) noz would they bœ perswaded to the contrary, vntill two of our Factozs went on shoze, and fully satis-
fied them in any thing they demanded oz doubted, and
that our intent was onely to make pzouision foz such
things as wee wanted, and the next mozning. (as the
manner there is) wee discharged another pœce of Ozdnance. And then the Gouernour of the Towne sent
a boate to know what we craued, whereupon wee certified them of our wants, and they told vs they would
giue the Gouernour intelligence, and returne vs an
answere, which was, that vnlesse wœ came into the
roade, it was beyond his Commission to relœue vs,
yet hauing first swozne and examined our Factozs,
and so knowing the truth of our intended voyage, they
gaue them a warrant to take a boate, to come a booze at
their pleasures with licence to supply our wants, if
they

they had any thing that might content vs. Yet one
thing aboue the rest made vs much to maruell , which
was , two English ships (which wee perceiued and
knew by their flagges) being in the road, who had not
somuch kindnesse in them as to giue vs notice, of the
custome or manners of these subtill and currish people. And of this doubt , wee were also resolued,
that no man whatsoeuer, being once within their Dominions, may comeaboord any ship, that shall arriue
there,and lie out of the roade, although they bee of their
owne Nation , without their Gouernors and Coun-
cels permittance or licence.At our being there some
of them came aboord of vs euery day for the space of
fiue daies that we staied there, and eate and dranke
with vs , after an vnsatiable manner, and very gree-
dily. Also we sent the Gouernor a present of two chee-
ses , a Gammon of bacon, and fiue or fixe barrels
of pickled Oisters , which he accepted very thankefully,
and returned vs in requitall thereof, two or three Goats
and a Shæepe or two , and good store of Onions. And
there wee tooke in fresh water , Canarie wine, Mar-
malad of Quinces at twelue pence the pound, little
barrels of Suckets at three shillings the barrell, O-
ranges, Limmons, Pomecitrons and excellent faire
whit bread made with Anniseedes,and is by them called
Nunnes bread.

The eighteenth day of Aprill about seauen of the
clocke in the morning, wee waighed ancor and set saile,
hauing a Nice gale of winde for some three houres,and
being then becalmed,we houered to and fro till the 21.
day,and hauing then againe a faire gale of winde, wee
sailed vntill the 27.day about two or three of the clocke
in the afternoone, that we ariued and ancored at Mayo,
being about three hundred leagues from the Canaries,
and comming from thence, wee were determined to
take in fresh water at a place called Bonauista, but hauing ancored,wee found the water to bee two or three

miles, vp in the land, neither was it cleare water, so that we tooke the smaller quantity. But there were other good commodities: For at our first comming we were told by two Negroes, that there wee might haue as many Goats as we would, gratis, and I well remember, we had to the number of two hundred, or thereabouts in both our ships. Also they told vs that there were but twelue men in the Iland, and that there was verie great store of Salt growing out of the ground, so that (if we pleased) we might lade both our ships therewith: it is excellent good white salt, and as cleare as euer I saw any in England.

Ouer against the Ile of Mayo, some eight leagues distance, is an Iland called S. Deago; wee Caied at Mayo from the twenty seuenth of Aprill in the afternoone, vntill the fourth day of May at three of the clocke in the morning, when we set saile and sailed vntill the twentieth day of May, that we were past the Equinoctiall line, about 4. or 6. of the clocke in the morning, being distant frō the Ile of Mayo about three hundred fourty eight leagues or thereabouts, as our master Philip de Groue noted it downe in his owne Booke of the description of the whole Voiage. And thence wee still sailed forwards vntill the fourth of July, that wee came to a part of Souldania with all our men in health, Gods name be praised, but two which were touched a little with the scuruy, which soone after recouered themselues on shore to their former health.

Also the same day we espied Land which is called, Cape bona Speranse, being some fiftone or fifteene leagues off Souldania, and standeth in some thirty fiue Degres or thereabouts.

At Souldania wee refreshed our selues excellently well so long as we were there, and had, and tooke in for our prouision about foure hundred head of Cattell, as Oxen, Steeres, Sheepe and Lambes, and Fowles, and fish of sundry sorts very plentifull, and fresh water.

ter, great store. Also in that place is an Iland called
Pengwin, some fiue or sixe leagues from the maine
Land, where are great store of fowles called also Pen-
gwins, infinite number of Seales: And to fetch some
of those Seales, wee went twice thither and filled our
boate each time, and made traine Oile thereof for
Lampes. Also in this Iland we found 10. fat sheepe,
being left there by the Hollanders, for a Pinnis which
we met some two hundred leagues from Cape bona
Speranse, which sheepe we tooke with vs, and left sixe
beasts or bullocks in their steads.

At our first comming to Souldania, wee began to
build or set vp our Pinnis, and launched her the fifth
day of September next following, and in seuen or
eight daies after, shee was rigged and ready in all
points to haue gone away, if any such necessity had
béene.

Souldania is within the Kingdome of Ethiopia.
Now the Ethiopians are by nature very bruttish or
beastly people, especially in their feeding. For I haue
seene them eate the guts & garbedge, yea euen the very
panch where the dung & filth lieth. Also when wo haue
cast off those Seale fishes into the riuer neere adioyning where they haue lyen the space of fourtéen daies,
and that they haue béene putrified and stuncke so vehe-
mently, that it could almost haue stifled one of vs to
come by them, these people haue taken them vp and
eaten them when they haue swarmed with crawling
maggots.

Also in this Countrey are sundry sorts of wilde
beasts, which my selfe and others of our Company
(going on shore of purpose) haue seene, and perceiued
some of them to be very fierce and cruell: so that afterwards when we found their dens, wo durst not enter them, nor come very neere them, lest they should
be in them.

The Ethiopians brought downe to the shore side to

sell Estriges egges and some empty shels, with a small
hole in one end, with Estriges feathers and Porpentines quils, and for all their Traffique and Commodities, they chiesely desire Iron, esteeming it more
then eyther gold or siluer. For with our old Iron, wee
bought all our Cattell, and any thing else that we had of
them.

In this Country we remained from the fourekenth
day of July, vntill the twentieth day of September then
next following.

The 20. day of September earely in the morning we
waighed ancor, and that night we lost the good ship called the Vnion, and our Pinnis called by the name of the
Good hope, the night being very darke and windy: now,
the euening before we lost them, the Vnion (about siue
of the clocke) put out her Ensigns, but to what intent
we knew not, nor could imagine, but all that night wee
lay at Hull.

The next day being the 21. day, hauing a faire and
strong gale of winde, and afterwards sundry contrary
windes and many calmes, yet at length wee attained to
the height of S. Laurence on the 27. day of October, standing in the height of 26. degrees, from whence we sailed
with many crosse and contrary winds, and calmes. Yet
at length on the 22. day of Nouember, in the morning
we descried two or three small Ilands, and in the afternoone wee espied an Iland called Gomora a very high
Land: and on the 24. day we sent our boate to the shore
side, and there came to the shore side siue or sixe men of
that Country, and sold vs Plantins, and nothing else at
that time.

The next day we sent our boate againe, but a little
before they came to the shore, they espied a Cannooe
and two men in it a fishing: wee went betweene them
and the shore but would not violently take them: then
we shewed them a knife or two, and they came both
into our boate, and we brought them aboord our Ship
and

and vſed them very kindly, and gaue one of them a
Turbant to put on his head, and to the other a little glaſſe
of a quarter of a pint full of Aquavitæ, and ſent them
a ſhore. From the 22. day that wee eſpied the Iland
Gomora, and came amongſt the Ilands, wee could haue
no ſteady gale of winds to carry vs forward, vntill the
25. day that with the winde and aid of our Pinnis which
towed our ſhip betweene the two Ilands adioyning to
the ſhore, wee came to an ancor that night betwixe
foure and fiue of the clocke in ſome 17. or 20. fathome
water.

The 26. day wee ſent our boate to ſhore with a
preſent to the King, by Maſter Iordan, who went himſelfe alone with the preſent, leauing onely a pledge or
two in the boate till his returne: The preſent was
a paire of Kniues: a Sabh or Turbant, and a looking glaſſe with a combe in it, to the value of ſome 15.
ſhiKings in all, which the King receiued ſomewhat
ſcornefully, not ſcarce looking on it, or at the leaſt
thinking it to bee but of ſmall value, and gaue it to one
of his Noble men, and told maſter Iordan our Factor,
that if our Generall would come on ſhore, hee ſhould
haue any thing that they had; and with this anſwere
hee departed: and at his comming from the King, the
King bowed himſelfe towards him in very courteous
manner, and after his departure (as it may ſeems) hee
better peruſed the preſent. For in the afternoone hee
ſent our Generall in requitall, a very fat young Bullocke, which wee receiued, and gratified the meſſen-
gers with a couple of penny kniues, wherewith they
thought themſelues very royally contented. The
27. day our Generall went on ſhore and ſome 12.
with him, and carried with him a ſmall banquet: as
a boxe of Marmaled, a barrell of Suckets, and Wine,
which they did eate befor the King but hee would neither eate nor drinke, but his Nobles did both eat and
drinke. And after the banquet, hauing ſome conference

with

with the King by his Interpreter concerning our
wants, by whom wee vnderstood, that they had some
dealings with the Portugals, of which language hee
could speake a little, which was sufficient to satisfie vs
with what they had.

The 28. day the King had determined to come a-
boord of our Ship, but his Interpreter told vs, that his
Councell and the common people would not suffer him
so to doe. Also that day towards night I went ashore
where our people were cutting downe wood, and came
aboord againe with the boat.

The 29. day I went ashore againe, with our Master,
Master Tindall, Master Iordan, and our whole noyse
of Trumpeters, and at the shoreside were very kindly
entertained by the Interpreter, who brought vs to the
King, being then by his Palace side, who at our approch
bowed himselfe vnto vs very courteously. Hee hath
for his guard when he walketh abroad fixe or eyght men
with kniues of a foote long, and as broad as hatchets
and very sharpe, which goe next to his per'on, and more
goe before him, and many behinde him, to keepe and defend him, from what iniury or wrong soeuer may come
or happen.

These people seeme to bee ciuill, kinde, and true-
hearted to strangers, for in going two and fro, ashore
and aboard, one of our men carelesly left his sword
behind him at night when hee came aboord, which being found by one of the people of Gomora, hee brought
it to the King, who perceiuing it to bee some of ours,
demanded how hee came by it? who answered, hee
found it, and the King againe told him, that if hee pro-
ued the contrary, it should cost his best blood: the next
day at our comming on shore, the Kings Interpreter
brought vs the sword, and told vs the Kings pleasure
therein.

Also they seeme to haue a very ciuill gouernment
amongst them, for at their meeting in the morning,
they

they will shake hands each with other, and speake one to another, which to vs seemed to bee their kinde and friendly salutations one to another. They are very modest, streight, big-limmed, and very comely in gesture both men and women. Their Religion Mahometicall, and goe almost naked, onely their priuities are couered with linnen cloth, and Turbants on their heads.

The women haue a linnen cloth, that couereth their brests before, and reacheth to the middle, and from the middle to the knee and somewhat lower, they are couered round about with linnen neere to their shin, and sedges tied round about them like a rowle at their waste, and hang downe, which doth become them very well.

They goe all barefoot except the King, who hath a paire of soles on his feet: and for his apparell when I saw him, he had a white wrought networke Cap, a Scarlet wastecote loose about him, and open before, with sleeues, and a linnen cloth about his middle, and another which hanged downe from his shoulders to his feet.

Also at our being there at the Towne, they brought vs Coquo nuts to sell, as bigge as a mans head, and round, and some bigger and some lesser, with water in them according to the proportion or bignesse of the shell, and as much meat in one shell as would suffice for a mans dinner.

Also they brought vs Goats, Hens, Chickens, Limmons, Rice, Milke, Fish, and such like, which wee bought for Commodities, as two hens for a penny knife, Limmons, and Coquo nuts for old Iron, as nailes, broken pikes, and such like. But for fresh water there is small store, and that they haue, is gotten out of the sands, viz. First, they make a hole in the sands, and when the water commeth into the hole, they take it out into their Coquo shels and so drinke

C   it.

it.   They brought vs of that water, but none of our
company would drinke thereof, it looked so thicke and
muddy.

In this Iland of Gomora we stayed from the 25. day
of Nouember vntill the 29. of the same, and then wee
waighed ancor and departed.

The tenth day of December about two or three of
the Clocke in the morning, and the Moone shining,
weespied on a sudden a lowland with high trees growing by the shore side, we being not aleague from the
shore, so that if we had not espied the trees, we should
haue thought the land to haue bene but the shadow of
the Moone, and so might haue run our selues on shore,
and cast our selues away with ship and goods: but it
was Gods good prouidence thus to defend vs from
so great and emment danger, whose name be blessed
at oprad eunoto and euermore.

This was the Iland of Pemba, which wee tooke to
be Zirzabar, vntill by one of the people of the Countrie we foundit to be Pemba. At the sight of this low
Iland, after we plainely perceiued it, wee presently
tacke about and set from the shore till day, and then
we tackt about againe to the shore side, and neering
alongst the shore side for a harbour to ancor in, wee
sent our Pinnis in the meane time, to the shore with
the Gang only and master Elmore to sake for a conuenient watering place, wee keeping our course till
our Pinnis came to the shore side. Then two or three
of the people of the Iland demanded in the Portugall
language what wee were, and one of our men made answer, that we were Englishmen. Then they demanded againe what we had to doe there, in regard the
King of Portugall was King of that Iland: wee
replied, that wee knew not so much, neither came
we thither for any euill intent whatsoeuer, but only
to water, and would giue them satisfaction for any o-
ther thing that we should haue of them. Then it drew

towards

towards night, and our men came aboozd and acquainted the whole Company with this their party on
shoze.

The 11. day our boat went ashoze to the same
place, but found it void of people and returned, and
presently we came to an anchor, about fiue oz sixe of the
Clocke in the afternoone, neere vnto two oz three broken Ilands there, adioyning neere to the maine Iland
of Pemba. This place of our then ancoring standeth in
the height of fiue Degrees and 10. minutes.

The 12. day our Pinnis went on shoze to the same
place, with master Iordan, one of our Merchants. At
whose comming on shoze, after some conference with
some that could speake Portugall, but not with those
(as it seemed) with whom we spake the day befoze,
foz these told master Iordan the King was a Mallaibar,
and after some other conference, master Iordan told
them, that although our ship were an English ship, yet
he was a Portugall Merchant, and the goods in the
ship were Portugals goods. Then they told vs wee
should not want foz any thing they had: and hereupon
they sent a Moore into our boat to make search foz a
conuenient watering place, who after some small
search, bzought vs to a little hole at the bottome of
a hill, being hemmed in with the hill on the one side,
and a ditch on the other side, there we filled our barre-
coes, and being ready to goe aboozd, wee desired the
Moore to goe aboozd with vs, who willingly agreed
thereto, and we vsed him very kindly, till the next
mozning that we went to water againe, and carried
him on shoze with vs, by whose report of his kinde v-
sage aboozd, there came downe with him another
that could speake a little Portugall, who (as hee said)
was one of the Kings Gentlemen: him wee also
bzought aboozd and vsed him very kindly, and set
him ashoze the next day: Who pzomised at his departure to bzing vs Hennes, Coquenuts, and Oren-

C 2   ges,

ges, which hee did accordingly, and then our Master,
with master Reuer and my selfe went ashore with
some others of the Company, where wee dined, and
after dinner came two Caualliers, and a Moore being
one of their slaues, to the watering place, where our
men were filling of the Caske, and asked whether there
were any of the chiefe of our ship, or Company there:
To whom Edward Churchman one of our Company
made answere, and said there was our Master, and one
of the Merchants, whom (if it pleased them) hee would
bring to parle with them: and at their meeting, they
saluted each other after the Portugall manner. And after
some Conference, demanding what we were, wee told
them we were Englishmen: and they replied that wee
were very welcome, and all that they had, or the Iland
could afford, was at our command and disposing: to
whom wee gaue hearty thanks.

But these sugred words of theirs, were only in outward shew, to cloake their treacherous practices, as af-
terward we found it true.

Then we demanded what they were? and it was answered, that one of them was the kings brother, who
instantly shewed vs a siluer ring, whereon was ingra-
uen the number of villages, and houses, or cottages in
the Iland, and said he was Ruler and Gouernor of all
those places. Then wee asked them, if there were any
Portugals in the Iland? they sayd no, for they had
banished them all, because they would haue reliefe
there perforce, and would make slaues of the people
of the Iland, (which being not able to indure) they
made continuall warres with them at their comming
hither.

In the meane time, our Pinnis came on shore,
which had beene at another place of the Iland for Cattell according to appointment, but were deferred off,
till they might get fitter opportunity for their intended
treachery.

                                              Then

Then our men told vs that they had heard of that side of the Iland where they were for Cattell, that is, saile of Hollanders had lately taken Mossemberge, and put all the Portugals to the sword: which newes they had heard from Zinzibar to bee true: whereat these Caualliers seemed outwardly to reioyce, which was also another subtill traine to bring vs within compasse of their intended treachery. And when night drew on, we intreated them to goe aboord with vs, which then they refused to doe, but promised to come aboord the next day, being the seuenteenth day of December: which the Kings brother (as hee named himselfe) did with two others: but before they came aboord, they craued pledges, which they had, viz. Thomas Caue, Gabriel Brooke, and Laurence Pigot our Surgeon. The other three being then aboord, wee vsed them verie kindly vntill they went on shore, on the eighteenth day in the morning: And our Generall gaue the chiefe of them two Coats, a paper Cartridge of Gunpowder, and some other small trifles to the other two, and so went on shore, and master Reuer, master Iordan, M. Glascot and my selfe went with them for our pledges, and at our comming on shore and fearing no treachery, wee went fiue or eight vnaduisedly vp to the houses for our pledges, whom we found guarded with fifty or sixty men armed with seuerall weapons, as Bowes and Arrowes, Swords and Bucklers, Darts, and Cuttleares: yet at our comming thither, wee receiued our pledges, and without longer stay, departed to the Sea side, accompanied with the Kings brother: and immediately most of those Moores came also after vs, and fiue or eight of them came to our Pinnis side and viewed her, and so departed againe to the rest of their fellowes.

And we instantly entered our boat, and intreated the Kings brother to go aboord with vs, which hee willingly did, and we entertained him with all kindnes that we

C 3 could,

could, vntill it was night that we was to depart, when
our Master offered him a knife, with some other odde
trifles, which he scornfully refused, and presently went
ashoare in our boat: Vpon this, we mistrusted some treachery intended against vs; and therefore thought to bee
better armed at our next comming ashoare.

The 19 day our Long-boat went ashore in the morning verie early, to fill our Caske with water, and hauing filled the same within a litle, they espied our sailes
out, being let downe to dry, but they imagined we were
going away: Whereupon the companion to y Kings brother came to our Boatswaine, and asked him if we were
going away? The Boat-swain, as well as he could, both
by signes and otherwise, told him, it was only to dry
our sailes. And as they were thus talking, they espied our
Pinnace comming, being then very well armed, and left
off making any further inquiry; which Pinnace had they
not then espied, it was likley they had intended to haue
cut off our men, & taken our boat; for there were two of
these Rogues at the least lying in ambush about the watering place, readie to haue giuen the onset, if the watchword had been giuen. By this time our Pinnace was
come to the shore, and our men standing on their gard
vpon the sants, not farre from her, then our Master sent
Nicholas White, one of our gang, to tell them of y Iland,
that our Merchants were come on shoare, who passing by
one of their houses, might perceiue the same to be full of
people, & amongst the rest, fir Portugals in long bran-
ched damaske Coats, lined with blue taffata, and vnder
the same, white callico breeches. This Nicholas White, at
his returne told vs: and presently came downe the companion to the Kings brother, and told Master Reuer, the
Merchants were weary, and intreated them to go vp to
the to see the Cattell, which was only one bullock which
Nicholas White saw at his going vp, and no more. But
Master Reuer craued pardon, desiring him to send downe
the Bullocke, & there were commodities in the boat to

make

make satisfaction for the same. With this answer, and seeing vs better armed then we were wont to bee, he went away. The Kings brother being then on the sands, commanded a Negro to gather Coquanuts to send to our Generall, & made choise of Edward Churchman one of our men, to fetch the same, whom we neuer saw after, nor could euer know what became of him; But when they saw that none of vs would come ashore, but stood vpon our gard, they gaue the watchword and sounded a horne, and presently set vpon our men at the watering place, and slew Iohn Harrington, the Boat-swains man, & wounded Robert Buckler, Master Elanors man very sore, with 8. or 10. mortall wounds, and had killed him, but that we discharged a Musket or two, which (as it seemed) hurt some of them; for then they retired: in which meane time (though weake and faint) he did at length recouer our boat. Also two or three more of our men by creeping, and lying close in the ditch, vntill they espied our boat, got also safe aboord; and then counting our men, we only missed Edward Churchman, and Iohn Harrington, that was slaine: and so comming aboord, we certified the company of all our proceedings on shoare; and our Surgeon dressed Robert Buckler, and after, did his best for his cure and recouery of his health.

The twenty day in the morning we went on shoare with our Pinnace and Long-boat, very well armed to fetch in our Dauid (which is a piece of wood or timber where with we hale vp our Ancor.) and a little beyond the same, we found Iohn Harrington dead, and starke naked, whom we buried at another Iland, hard by the maine Iland.

The naturall people of the Iland Pemba, seeme to be louing and kind: for they made signes to me and others, at our first comming, to beware of our throats cutting: which then we tooke no heede or notice of, vntill this their treachery put vs in minde thereof againe.

The same day (being the 20. day) we waighed Ancor,

and about 11. of the clocke at night, our ship was on
grounde on the sholds of Meluidee, or Pemba, which
we certainly knew not: Yet God of his mercy, (as
formerly in the late pretended treacherie, so in that
extremity) did mightily defend and preserue vs,
whose name bee praised and glorified now and euermore.

The 13. day in the morning, wee espyed three saile
being small boats, slightly wrought together, called
Pangaias, which we chased after and tooke: which they
on ship espying, they sent out an Almiloj, being also
a Pangaia, which perceiued that wee had taken the o-
ther, and returned to the shore.

Now of those which we had taken, there were some
6. or 8. of the chiefest that were thought by our company to be Portugals, the rest being certainly knowen
to be Moores, and were in all some fourty and odde
persons, and those sixe or eight were pale and white,
much differing from the colour of the Moores. Yit
being asked, what they were, they said, they were
Moores and shewed vs their backes all written with
Characters; and when we affirmed them to be Portugals, they then told vs, the Portugals were not circum-
cised.

But to conclude, our Company would not be perswaded but that they were Portugals: then some of
our Company told them of all the intended treacheries,
with the losse of three of our men, and wounding of
the third, which made them fearefull of our revenge,
(as it seemed) and then they talked together in their
owne language, which made vs also suspect some vil-
lanous and desperat attempt to be pretended by them,
and therefore, I kept my selfe still vpon the poope,
and looked carefully to the swords which stood naked-
ly in the Masters Cabbin, which they also knew and
noted, and marked Master Glascock and my selfe,
where we set our swords, still expecting to haue the
place

place downe, which I perceiuing, kept good watch,
left greater hurt should ensue thereby, and being thus
alone on the poope, they beckened me three or foure seuerall times to come to them vpon the space Decke, which
I denied, left they should so recouer the swords, whereby far more hat me might haue beene done, then afterwards was done.

When our Master came vpon the spare decke and
demanded, which was their Pilot, whom hee tooke
downe into his Cabbin, and shewed him his plat,
which hee at his comming downe did very earnestly
behold.

But at his going from thereft with our Master, he
spake in the Moores language, warning them (as we
thought) to looke to themselues, and doe their best a-
mongst vs, and to giue eare when he gaue the watchword and then to giue the Onset.

Also there were speaches vsed that the Pilot had a
knife about him, and being searched for it, he nimbly
conueied the same from the one side to the other, and
therewith suddenly stabbed the Master into the belly, &
then cried out, which (belike) was the Watchword:
For then they began the onset on the spare decke,
where Master Glascocke, Master Tindall, our Generall, and one or two more with them chanced to kill
foure or fiue of the white Rogues, and made such ha-
uocke among the reft, that at length they had slaine al-
moft fourty of them, and brought the reft in fubiec-
tion.

Now, a little before our Master thus called the Pilot, he entreated our Generall, that if they had any
garuances or peason (being their Country sow) they
would let vs haue some, which they should be paid for,
& what was taken from them, should be restored,
with free liberty to go where they would: whereto the
Generall confented, & heereupon our Master called the
Pilot, to see if he had any skill in the Plat, and so to let

him

him depart, and all the rest. But when thus treacherously they offered vs the first abuse, we could doe no lesse then we did, being in our owne defence, and for the safegard of our liues.

Yet did some fiue or sixe of these villaines recouer a Pangaia by their excellent swiftnesse in swimming, and escaped to the shore, they swimming to windward, faster then our Pinnis could rowe.

In this skirmish were hurt but three of our Company, namely, master Glascocke, with two wounds, whereof one was a deepe wound in his backe, master Tindals was aimed at his brest, he hauing nothing in his hand to defend himselfe, yet by the assistance of the Almighty, hee turned himselfe about and receiued the stabbe in his arme, and our Masters was in his belly, as is formerly sayd, which (God be thanked) they all recouered and were well curd.

The 19. day of Ianuary wes espied many Ilands, which the Portugals call by the name of Almailant, being to the number of nine Ilands, all vnpeopled as the Portugals write and affirme.

The 20. day we sent our Pinnis in the morning to one of those Ilands to seeke fresh water, but could find none: yet they found there great store of Land Turtles, and brought some sixe aboord: then we sailed to an other Iland, which seemed more likely for fresh water then the first, where we cast ancor.

The 21. day about ten of the Clock in the forenoone, riding there at twelue or thirteene fathome water, and a reasonable good harbour, wee stayed there vntill the first day of February, and then waighed ancor, and departed. Here we refreshed our selues very well with fresh water, Coquo nuts, Fish, Palmitoes, and Doues great plenty.

The first day of February, we set saile, and sailed with a faire winde vntill the 19. day, that wee passed the Equinoctiall line, and on the fifteenth day in the

morning

mozning betime, we came within ken of land, which was the coast of Melucidey vpon the maine.

The 16. day we came to an Ancoz, about nine of the Clocke in the mozning, at 12. fathome water, and some two leagues from the shoze, and pzesently wee sent our Pinnis to the shoze to seeke some refreshing, but they could by no meanes get on shoze; noz would the people of the Country (being fearefull) come within parly, which at their retarne they certified our master of, and so in the afternoone we set saile againe, and departed.

Now about this time it pleased God, (by the confession of William Aston, one of our ship boyes) to reueale a foule and detestable sinne committed amongst vs; which being appzoued against him by a Iury, hee was condemned to die, and was executed foz the same on the third day of March (being Friday) in the mozning.

The 21. day betimes in the mozning, we espied an Iland standing in the height of 12. Degrees and 17 minutes, being barren and vnpeopled, euer against which Iland, some thzee leagues distant, stood foure hillocks oz rocks. & foz this Iland wee boze vp a whole day and a night, and finding it to bee barren and vnpeopled, by sending our skiffe on shoze, wee passed by it, and the same day we espied thzee Ilands moze about sunne setting, standing in the height of 12. Degrees and 39 minutes, to which Iland wee came the 29. day of March. 1609, two of which Ilands were within a league one of another, and the third we found to be Sacatora, and standeth in 12. Degrees and 24. minutes, where we Ancozed in a fine Bay the 30. day in the mozning about ten of the Clocke.

At sight of vs, the Ilanders made a fire, and wee sent our skiffe on shoze, but the people fled with great feare and trembling, hauing (as it seemes) beene foz merly iniured by some that had passed that way: but our men looking about, found no likely-hood of any re-lile there, and so came aboord and certified the Gene-rall thereof: so that about fiue of the clocke in the after-noone, wee waighed ancor, and sailed along to finde out the chiefe harbor.

The 31. day wee stood off into the maine Sea, where we met with a Guzarat ship, laden with Cotton wools, Callicoes, and Pentathors, being bound for Adden, whither wee kept her company, in regard they told vs it was a Towne of great trading, but wee found it quite contrary: for it was onely a Towne of garison, and many Souldiers in it: and at the very en-tring into the Towne, is a Castle cut out of the maine, and incompassed round with the Sea, wherein are thir-ty two peeces of Ordnance, and fifty peeces in the Towne.

The 10. day of Aprill wee arriued there, and the Guzarat ship went into the Towne, and told the Go-uernour, there was an English Ship come to trade there. Who presently sent his Admirall to vs, and our Generall vnaduisedly went on shore, where hee, and his fellowes were receiued with 4. great Horses, and were carried before the Gouernour, in as great pompe and state, as the Towne could yeald. But the Gouernour finding him to be a plaine and simple man; put him in a house with a Chowse or keeper, with ma-ny Ianyzaries or Souldiers to gard him, and so kept him prisoner the weeke, my selfe being prisoner with him.

And then the Gouernour caused him to send aboord for Iron, Tinne, and Cloth, to the value of 1500. Dollars, with promise to buy the same: which when he had on shore, he claimed and made stay thereof, for the Custome of the ship onely: and when hee saw he had gotten as much as hee could, hee sent him aboord the 27. day of May, and kept 2. of our merchants for 2000. Dollars, which he said was for ancorage: but the Ge-

nerall

uerall voice of the company was, that hee should haue
none: whereupon hee sent the Marchants vp into the
Countrey some 8. daies iourney, to a place called Siz-
ny, where the Basshaw then lay.

The 28 day, our Pinnace came to vs, who told
vs their Master was dead: and inquiring where, and
how, the company told vs, he was knockt in the head
with a Mallet hammer, by one Thomas Clarke, with
the consent of Francis Driuer his mate, Andrew Euans,
and Edward Hilles, beeing foure murderous and bad-
minded men: who beeing asked why, and vpon what
occasion they did it, they could make no excuse, nor al-
ledge any cause, saue only, that hee had some small
quantity of Aqua vitæ and Rosa solis for his owne
store, and for the good of them, or any one aboord, that
should stand in neede thereof, and was prouident to
keepe and preserue the same, till great need should be,
and therefore out of meere malice, and chiefly by the
instigation of Francis Driuer his mate, they thus mur-
dred an innocent man, who thought them no harme,
nor suspected any such danger.

The 31. day of May, a Iury was called, and vpon
iust and due proofe, according to our English lawes,
they were conuicted, and Francis Driuer and Thomas
Clarke were condemned and iudged to die, and were
hanged in the Pinnace where they did the fact: and on
the other two, God shewed his iust iudgement afterwards. For Edward Hilles was eaten with Caribs
or Man-eaters, and the other died and rotted where
hee lay.

The third day of Iune, wee weighed ancer and sailed into the Red-sea, thorow the straights of Mockoo;
which are some league ouer from shore to shore, and 18.
fathome water, close aboord the Iland shore, and a-
bout 3. leagues in length.

When you are within the Straits, there lieth a
great shole, some two leagues off into the Sea, and to

The master of the Pinnace murdered.

D 3   shun

shunne it, you must take a good breath off, and so you shall come in no danger, and then you haue to Mockoo some 6. leagues, where is a good Road to ancor in and faire ground, and you may ride at 14 fathome water. It is a place that is neuer without shipping, for it is a Towne of great trade of merchandize, and hath Carauans or Connoyes that come from Seena, from Mecha, from grand Cairo, and Alexandria, and all those places.

Moha sixe leagues within the Straits,

It is a City of great trading for our Commodities: as Tynne, Iron, Lead, Cloth, Sword blades, and all English commodities. It hath a great Bussart or Market euery day in the wicke. There is great store of fruit, as Apricocks, Quinses, Dates, Grapes abundance, Peaches, Limmons, and Plantirs great store, which I much marueller at, in regard the people of the Country told vs, they had no raine in seuen yeres before, and yet there was very good Corne and good store, for eightene pence a bushell.

There are Oxen, Sheeps, and Goats abundance: as an Oxe, for 3. Dollars, a Goat for halfe a Dollar, and a Sheepe for halfe a Dollar: as much Fish for three pence, as will soffice ten men to a meale : As Dolphines, Wore-fish, Basse, Mullets, and other good Fish.

The Town is Arabian, and gouerned by the Turk, and if an Arabian offend, hee is seuerely punished by their Law. For they haue Gallies and Chaines of purpose, which offenders are put into, else were they not able to keepe them in awe and subiection.

Their abode at Moha.

At Mockoo, wee staid from the 23. of Iune, till the 18. of Iulie, and then waighed ancor, and went out to the mouth of Mockoo, where wee lost two ancors, and from thence wee set saile to Sacatora : and about the 5. of August, wee cast ancor ouer against the Towne of Saiob, where the King lieth, and one of our Merchants went on shore and gaue the King a present, and desired that

that we might buy Water, Goats, and other prouision, which hee would not grant, because the women of
the Country were much afraid: yet hee told him, if hee
would goe to a Road some fiue leagues off, wee should
haue any thing his Countrey would affozd: where we
bought Goats, Water, Aloes Socotrina, Dragons
bloud, and what else the Countrey would affozd.

Heere at Sawb, wee remained from the 5. day of August, till the 18. day, and set saile with an anco3 and a
halfe, fo2 Cambaia.   And on the 28. day of August, we
came to Mo3, where one of the Country people told
vs, that fo2 the value of 10. Dollars, wee might haue a
Pilot to b3ing vs to the bar of Surot. But our willfull
Master refused it, and said he would haue none.

The 29. day wee set saile from thence, thinking to
hit the Channell to goe to the bar, but wee came out of
10. fathome water into 7. fathome, and into sire fathome and a halfe. Then we tackt about to the West-
ward, and came into 15. fathome, and then wee tackt
about againe to the Eastward, and came into 5. fathome water. Then some of the companie asked whither the Master would goe? who answered, Let her go o-
uer the bright, and p3esently the ship strooke, which I
p3esently went vp and told him of: who turning about,
asked who durst say shee strooke? then p3esently shee
strooke againe, and strooke off her Rudder, and left it
in the Sea: then wee came to an anco3, and rode there
two daies, then our Skiffe split in pieces, and wee had
no mo3e but our long boat to helpe our selues withall:
yet we made such shift, that wee got the pieces of our
skiffe into the ship, and the Carpenter went so round-
ly to wo3ke, that they had bound her vp together with
woldings, so that when our greatest need was, shee
b3ought 16. men on sho3e.

The second day of September about sir of the clock   The ship
at night, our ship strooke and began to sounder, and   foundreth
hauing strooke twice, we had p3esently 24. inches of
water

water in the Well, then we plied the pumpe, some foure houres, viz. from seuen of the Clocke to eleuen of the Clocke at night, then the water encreased so fast, that we were able to keepe her no longer, but were forced to take our boats.

The Merchants had some 10000. l. lying betweene the maine Mast and the Stearige, whereof the Generall bid the Company take what they would, and I thinke they tooke amongst them some 3000. pounds, some hauing 100. pounds, some 50. pounds, some 40. pounds, some more, and some lesse, and so we left the ship, and tooke neither meat nor drinke with vs. And betweene twelue and one of the Clocke, we set saile to come ashore, which was at the least 20. leagues to the Eastward, and so we sailed all that night, and the next day, without any sustenance at all, till fiue or six of the Clocke at night, being the third day of September, that we made to Land, being a little Island, standing vpon the bar, and then a gust came down vpon vs, & broke the midship thought of our long boat, wherein were 55. persons, yet it pleased God that we recouered our Mast, and (the gust ceasing) we went ouer the barre, and got into the Riuer of Gandeuee.

Gandeuee River.

But when the Country people saw so many men in two boats, they strooke vp their drums and were in Armes, taking vs to be Portugals, and that wee came to take some of their Townes: which wee perceiuing, (and hauing by chance a Guzarat aboord, wee sent him ashore to tell them truly what wee were : and when they knew we were Englishmen, they directed vs to the City of Gandeuee, where was a great Gouernour, who at our comming thither (and vnderstanding we were Englishmen) seemed to be very sorry for our misfortunes, and welcomed vs very kindly. And there ended our trauels by Sea for that time.

1609.

The fourth day of September, 1609. we came to the City of Gandeuee, which is a very faire hauen, and

and great store of shipping built there, whereof some are of foure or fiue hundreth Tun, it standeth in a good Soile, and is gouerned by the Gentiles.

The 25. day of September, we tooke our iourney towards Surror, to a Towne called Sabay, which is a Towne, only consisting of Spinners and Weauers, and there is much Calico made; and from thence we came to Surrate, where we found one William Finch an English Merchant, and seruant to Master Iohnson in CheapSide, who very courteously went to the Gouernour, and acquainted him with our distresse, who (as hereafter we found it to be true) was bribed by the Portugals, which told him we were a kinde of turbulet people that would make mutinies, and sow ciuill dissention in the Towne, and so aduenture to surprise the Towne, whereupon we were put into a Monastery where we liued three daies, nor could this suffice, but we were remoued to a great house, being a Gentiles house, where we lay 14. daies; in which time, (by the good aduice of the said William Finch) we made prouision of Coaches, Horses and other things to trauell to the great Mogol, & certifie him of our great distresse and missfortunes. This is a City of great fame & Antiquity, being walled about with free stone, and a strong Garrison lying therin, and a City of great trading for Merchandize, and great store of shipping, wherof some are of 500. Tun, which they cannot lade at the Town, but carry them ouer the bar with their ballace onely, & there lade thē, but for their smaller shipping, they lade them at the Town, and so goe ouer the bar, where at a high water, they haue 16. foot water.

The 23. of September, we tooke our iourney from Surrat to Agra, with our Generall and 57. men, with 21. Coaches of our owne, and some others being hired, and 19. Horses to a great City called Brámport, and the first two nights we lay in the fielos. _The trauell to Agra._

The 26. day we came to Nawbon, where Sugar groweth in abundance, with Cotton and all maner

C   of

of graine, as Rice, Wheat, Beanes, Pease, Chircoze, Lantæchoes, Motle,&c. Foz the Countrey is so plentifull, that you may haue a gallon of milke foz a halfe penny, a Hen foz thzee halfpence, & 16.Egs foz a penny.

From Gandence to Sabay is 12.course, & from Sabay to Surror is 12. course, and euery two course is thzee English miles.

The 27. day, we trauelled 12. course, and came to a City of the Bannians called Daytaotote, and theis Master Reuer one of our Merchants dico.

This City could neuer be conquered by the great Mogol, but yælded vpon compofition, and still holdeth his title of King of the Bannians, and at this City we staied two daies.

This City yældes great stoze of Dzugs, fine Pentathoes and Calico Lawnes.

The first of October we trauelled 12. course, and lay in the fields.

The second day we trauelled 14. course to a great City of the Bannians called Netherberry, where is a great Basar oz Market, and all maner of bzozen wares to be sold, as Pots, Kettles, Candlesticks, and Caldzons of foure fot long, Shirts of Male, Swozds and Bucklers, Lances, Hozses in Armour of Arrowe pzofe, Camels, and all manner of beasts.

There is also great stoze of Cotton wools, Cotton yarne, Pentathoes, Callico Lawnes, Shashes foz Turbants foz their heads, Limmons, Potatoes, thzæ pound foz a penny, and all maner of Dzugs.

And surely cloth would be a very vendible commodity there : foz coorse felt is there extreme deare. Also Gold and Siluer is there very plentifull, and these are very good people to deale withall.

The third day we trauelled ten course, to a small Towne of Husbandzy called Sailote, where is also great stoze of Sugar, and fruits of all sozts.

The next day we trauelled 18 course to a Garrison
Towne

Towne called Saddisce, and there is the Riuer of Tyn-
dee, which runneth to Surrat, wherein is great store of
Fish ot allsorts, and this Riuer diuideth the confines
of the Bannians and the Guzarates.

The Bannims are a strange people in their beliefe,
and honour God in a strange fashion, viz. in pictures
of stone, hanging their beades on the heads of the
pictures, and then with their faces towards the sun
doe worship it, saying, that all their comforts procede
from it. And yet I saw more then this, which was a
Cow adorned with a veste of gold and many Iewels,
her head bedecked with garlands and flowers, and
then being brought to a buriall place, where they doe
vse to make Sermons, they kisse her fæt and teats,
and worship her, that it grieued mæ to see their fond
superstition, and abominable Idolatry. And asking
why they did it, they answered, that shee was the mother of beasts, and brought them milke, butter, chæse,
and the Ore to till the ground, and lastly, her hide did
make leather to make them shoes. Moreouer, they
say, she is blest by the Mother of God, to be honoured
aboue all beasts. And so leauing the Bannians, wee
crossed the Riuer of Tindee into the Gentiles Countrey.

Now at Saddisce we being many, some in Coaches,
some on horseback, they thought we had come to take
their Town, and did shut their gates, & bent their Ordnance vpon vs. But our Generall sent our Linguist
or Interpreter to certifie them, what wæ were: and
then the Gouernour opened the Gates, and came
himselfe, to entertaine vs with great curtesse and state.
Yet that night we lay by the Riuer side and the next
day being the filth of October, we came into the
Towne, where we lay that night: And the next day
we trauelled some 12. Course, and lay at a Monastery:
And the seuenth day wæ went to the great City of
Bramport, where the great Generall called the Can

E 3   Canawe,

Canawe, liueth, this being his Garrison or resting place when he is out of the warres, and on the twelfth of October, hee came from the warres with 1500. Elephants, 30000. Horses, 10000, Camels, 3000. Drummedaries.

The Elephant serueth in the Field with a small tower of wood or timber vpon his back, wheron is placed 4. peeces of brasse as big as Kabuets, and 10. men very artificially placed in the said Tower, with bows and arrowes, and to discharge those peeces.

The Elephants skin is musket proofe, vnlesse it be on his face and belly, and he is a beast of so great vnderstanding, that he is ruled and gouerned by word of mouth, vnderstanding what his keeper commandeth him to doe.

This Country beareth toward the Northwest, in the height of 28. Degrées, or thereabouts. And here Muskets, Snap-hances, Pistols, Petronels, and Swords, be good commodities, but no Firelocks in any wise.

Also Cloth is an excellent commodity to my knowledge, for I was offered thrée pound for an old cloake, which heere is not worth 10. shillings at the vttermost.

And in Bramport we staied from the seuenth of October, vntill the 11. of Nouember following: When I, and Iohn Frencham one of our Company went to craue the Generals passe, to goe to the great Mogol: but he asked vs if we would serue him in his warres, and he would giue vs what meanes we would desire? but we told him, we were poore distressed mercharts, that had beene shipwracked: and he againe replied, that there was no Englishman, merchant, nor other but he was a Souldier. But we told him that we had wiues and childen in our Country, to whom we must of necessity goe: to which he sayd, It was very well spoken, and that it was against their Lawes to

keepe

kéepe any man against his will : Then he asked vs
if we had any Iewels for his Ladies ? I answered I had one stone and one Iewell, which I sold
him for fortie pound sterling, and then hée commanded his Secretary to make vs a Passe, and seale it
with his great Seale, for our safe Conduct to Agra.
Also for the nature and strength of the Elephant, I can
say thus much of mine owne knowledge because I
saw it:

An Elephant rolall being brought to remoue a piece
of Ordnance of one and twenty foot long, which
carried a shot of seuen inches high, and lay vpon the carriage on the side of a hill, and to carry the same some
halfe a furlong off; which he did, as it séemd, to the great
dislike of his Kéeper, who told him hes was a lazy vil-
laine, and deserued not his meat. Now the nature of
the Elephant is, not to be disparaged in any thing,
and standeth much vpon his reputation and valour:so
that vpon these spéeches of his Kéeper, he came to it a-
gaine, and with maine strength tore the carriage in
pieces, and left the peeces lying on the ground. Then
were Carpenters set on worke to make a new carriage, which being done, the same Elephant was broght,
who clapt his Trunke about the whéeles, and brought
the Ordnance where his Keeper commanded him.

This Citie is farre bigger than London, and great
trade of all sorts of merchandise therein: it is one of
the most famous heathen Cities that euer I came in,
and the Citizens are very good and kind people, and
very many Gallants in the Citie. Also fine riuers,
ponds, orchards, gardens, pleasant walkes, and excellent faire prospects as euer I saw. Heere any Gentleman may haue pastime to hunt or hawke : and if hee
will not goe farre, he may buy a Déere in the Busar or
market for a Doller, being but foure shillings sterling, and hunt him where and when he will.

Now in my iudgement, our English cloth of gold

and

and siluer, veluets, broad-cloth, bayes, and cottons, would be very vendible, in regard there are so many Gallants. And thus much for the great City of B..m-port.

The eleuenth of Nouember we took our iourny to-wards Agro, I and Ioseph Salebanck our Purser, and one Io. Frencham, with one of the Country people for our guide, taking leaue of our Generall, who was extreeme sicke of an Ague, and no hope of any speedy re-couery. Also we had thought to haue gone along with a Carrauand of foure hundred and fifty strong, which were bound for Agro: but the Captaine told vs, that they were to stay seuen daies longer; but said, if wee would trauell some two daies iourny (which we might safely doe without any danger of theeues) we should meet with a greater Carrauand then they were.

So on the twelfth day, we trauelled to a Towne called Caddor, some fifteene course from thence, where we lay that night.

Heere the Gouernor hearing that we were stran-gers, or Christians, demanded what we would haue, and whither we trauelled? We answered, to Agro, to the King, and that we came from Surrot. Then he as-ked vs what we would doe with the King? And when I heard him so inquisitiue, I peremptorily answered, that my businesse was too great for him to know: but he said, he would know it ere we went out of the Towne: and I againe replied, that my businesse was such, that I would goe out of the Towne and aske him no leaue: and so making vs ready to depart, we said, we would see who would stay vs, without a very law-full occasion. Then the Gouernor sent his Cotwall or the Maior of the Towne, who asked vs why we vsed such peremptory speeches to the Gouernor? We told him, We answered him in no worse manner then his place and calling deserued, and that it was not for him to force vs to acquaint him with our businesse to the King,

King, and then we shewed him the Can Carawes passe to the King. Whereupon the Gouernor came to vs again with twenty Gentlemen of the Towne, and by all meanes intreated vs to stay all night, and what-soeuer wee wanted that the Country could affoyd, should be at our seruice ; and withall told vs, the way was dangerous , and very bad to trauell.

The next day we gaue him halfe a pound of Tobac-co foy a pyesent , which wee byought out of England, which he accepted very thankfully.

The thirtentth day we came to a Towne called Sawbon, some 14 course from Caddor, but befoye we were halfe a course out of the Towne, the Gouer-nour sent 12. Hoysemen with Launces , Bowe and Arrowes, to conduct vs some part of the way that was most dangerous, which was some 10. oy 12. English miles.

And when we came to Sawbon, we found the Car-rauand being 500. Camels bound foy Agra, and were laden with Taffateis, wyought Silkes, Cloth, Sugar, and other Commodities, some from Bram-port, some from Bengalla, and some from Cambaia.

The 14. day we set foywards with the Carrauand, and trauelled some 12. course to a Monastery called Tindey.

The 15. day, wee trauelled some 10. course and lay in the woods.

The next day , we came to a great City called Can-nowe, where is much trading foy Cloth, Swoyds, Shashes, Peeces, and Armour tied on with strings, geing but onely Arrow pyoofe.

There is great stoye of fruit, and colonrs foy Di-ers, of all soyts : and I thinke our English cloth would be an excellent commodity there: foy it is very cold, es-specially in Ianuary, February and March, foy it bea-reth to the Noythwards.

The 16. day we trauelled some 14 course to a great River,

Riuer, called the Riuer of Andee, which is as bread as the Thames at Woolwich, and runneth into the Bay of Bengalla, and this is the vtmost part or border of the Gentiles, and on the 17. day we passed ouer the Riuer, and went out of the Gentiles Countrey.

The Gentiles will eat nothing that bleedeth, and the Sun is their great god; For, should they eat any thing that bleedeth, they beleeue that they may eat the soules of their Father, Mother, Sister, Brother, or friends, that are deceased: For, they say, that when any one dieth, their breath presently goeth into one beast or other, & so, in eating that beast, a man may eat the soule of some friend together with the flesh of that beast: such is their great blindenesse and ignorance. Nay more, they doe make euery liuing thing their Idols: as, the first liuing they meete in the morning, is their god or saint for that day, to worship that, and so leauing the Gentiles, we came to the Bulloits, or Pithagoreans.

The 17. day we came to the City of Gorra, where are many Surroyes, or Innes, where Trauellers may set their Camels, Horses or Cattell, and cost nothing.

Also there are foure great Schooles for learning, like to an Uniuersity: In this Countrey were two Brothers being Kings sonnes, who warred for this City, being eight miles in compasse, and in the middle a great wall, and there they laid their Seedge a long time. And at the last, the King of the East part got the victory, and held the same for seuen yeares, and then the great Mogol Tamberlaine the sixth ouercame the whole Countrey, and tooke it into his hands.

The 18. day, we went ten course to a great Tanch or poole of water, like vnto the Bath, the water boiling out of the earth and is very warme.

The 19. day, we trauelled some 15. course to a Towne called Sanday, where is great store of Wooll, like Spanish Wooll: heere are made great store of Caps to couer Turbants, felt gownes to ride in, both fine and

and courſe, there are great ſtore of ſhæpe, and ſo much Sugar, that they fæd horſes therewith as we do with prouender, alſo there are goodly Saraioes or Innes for horſemen and fœtmen.

The 20. day, wæ trauelled ſome fiftæne courſe to a great Surroy, neare vnto a Monaſtery, where wee had great ſtore of fruit called Mangres being like an Apple, and haue a ſtone as big as an Apricocke, and in ſent or taſte, and is excellent good for the Flire, and are there much eſtæmed of.

The 21. day we trauelled twelue courſe to a ſmall village, called Lee.

The 22. day we trauelled ſome 16. courſe to a City called Elman, where is a great Buſſart or Market for the countrey people, for Wooll, Cotton, Cotton yearne, Swords, Iauelins, and other weapons for the warres.

The 23. day, wæ came to a little Towne called Zirgreene, ſome 14. courſe, where is great ſtore of Wood, and aboundance of Drugs for Dyers.

The 24. day, we trauelled 16. courſe to a Citie called Barrandonn where are great ſtore of Merchauts of the Bannians and Meſulipatanians.

It is a City where the great Carrauans mæt, and there is great trade of Merchandiſe, for Cloth, Shaſhes, Armour, for men and Horſes, Coats of Male, Armour of Arrow proſe, bombaſt, Headpæces, and Elepharts tæth, alſo many wilde Elephants in the Countrey: here we ſtaied two daies and left our Carauant in the City.

The 27. day we tooke our iourney forwards, and by the way we met with a Con or Knight of that Countrey, with ſcuity Horſe being bound for Agro, and fifty ſhot, with whom we alſo kept company, being about 140. ſtrong, and trauelled in the Deſart ſome ſixe daies, where are great ſtore of wilde Elephants, Lions, Tygers, Cats of Mountaines, Porpentines,

F

penthres and other wilde beasts innumerable, but those wee saw. These Desarts are 100. course long, where euery night wee made great fires round about our tents, to shunne the dangers of the wilde beasts : This Con or Knight told vs the nature or wit of the Elephant, who knowing he is hunted to death for his teeth, will goe to a trée and there by maine force will wring or wrest his teeth out of his head, knowing that so he shall liue secure and frée from that danger, and this he protested to be true.

The third of December, we past those Desarts, and came to a Towne called Tranado.

The fourth day, we trauelled 16. course to a Towne called Zaioberbee, where is hay, corne, and graine, great plenty.

The fifth day we trauelled some 18. course to a City called Handec, where the King hath a Castle and house, cut out of the maine Rocke, and wrought with carued worke round about. This Castle is inuincible, and hath fifty péeces of Ordnance in it.

There lay in this Castle, when we were there, 200. Knights, Captaines, and other Gallants, that had transgressed the Law, or the Kings commandement, as in Treason, Rebellion, and such like matters. Also, in this City are two houses much like Saint Iones, where Captaines & Souldiers, that haue béen maimed, and hurt in the warres, doe liue, and haue each one a Mammothée a day, being nine pence English, and meat and drinke at the Kings allowance.

The 6. day we came to the Riuer of Tamluo, which runneth into the Riuer Indus, which parteth the Countries of the Pythagoreans, and the Indestans.

The Pythagoreans in former times haue béene a vile and treacherous kinde of people. and had a Law that when the husband died, the wife should hee also burnt, which is holden till this day, though not in so strict a manner, for now she may refuse it, but then

her

her head is shauen and she clad in a blacke vesture or garment, which among them is reputed most vile and hatefull, that the basest slaue in the Countrey will not succor nor releue her though she should starue.

Now, the cause why this Law was first made, was, for that the women there were so fickle and inconstant, that, vpon any slight occasion of dislike or spleene, they would poison their husbands. Whereas now the establishing and executing of this Law, is the cause that moueth the wife to loue and cherish her husband, and wisheth not to suruiue him.

As for example, I saw a young woman the wife of a Doctor whose husband being dead, she made choise to be carried in a Pageant, by foure men, she being clothed in Lawne, and her head decked with Iewels and rich Ornaments, and before her went Musicke of all sorts that the Coun'rey afforded, as Ha·boies, Drums, fifes, and Trumpets, and next vnto her all her kindred, and so shee was brought to the place of execution, where was a stake and a hole to set her feete in, and so being tied to the stake, all her kindred kneeling round about her, & praying to the sun & their other Idols, the fire was set to her, she hauing vnder each arme a bagge of Gunpowder, and a bagge betwixt her legges, and so burnt to death, the fire being made of Beniamin, Storaxe, Lignomaloes, and other swete woods. Thus much for the Bullocks, and so to the Indestands, and the next day we trauelled some ten course to a towne called A·lar.

The 8. day, we trauelled some 26. course, and came to the great City of Agro, where the great Mogoll keepeth his Court and residence.

The ni. th day Captaine Hawkins came to vs, and brought vs before the King, as it is the custome and manner of the Country. For no stranger must stay aboue twenty foure houres, before he be brought before the King, to know what he is, and wherefore hee commeth.

meth. Also euery ſtranger muſt preſent the King with ſome preſent bee it neuer ſo ſmall, which hee will not refuſe. And I gaue him for a preſent, a ſmall whiſtle of gold, waighing almoſt an ounce, ſet with ſparks of Rubies, which hee tooke and whiſteled therewith almoſt an houre. Also I gaue him the picture of Saint Iohns head cut in Amber and Gold, which hee alſo receiued very graciouſly.

The whiſtle hee gaue to one of his great women, and the picture to Sultane Caroone his yongeſt ſonne. His eldeſt ſon rebelled, and is in priſon with his eies ſealed vp, and it is noyſed amongſt the common people that his eyes are put out: But it was told mee by a great man, that they are but ſealed vp. His name is Patreſhaw Shelham, which in our language is heire apparant to the Crowne: His ſecond ſonne liueth with him and is called Sultane Mawbree, and him hee thinketh to make his heirs apparant. His third ſonne is called Sultane Lawlle, and is Viceroy of Lihorne: His fourth ſonne is called Sultane Lill, and is Viceroy of the Gentiles, and theſe are his fiue ſonnes. Alſo hee hath ten Viceroys more vnder him that gouern ten ſeuerall Prouinces or Countries, viz. Can Canow Viceroy of the Guzarats: Can Iohn Viceroy of the Bulloites: Michael Can Viceroy of the Bannians: Howſouer Can Viceroy of Cambaia: Hodge Iohn, Viceroy of Bengolla: Michael Can Viceroy of the Hendownes: Sawder Can Viceroy of the Putrans, and he lieth in the City of Candahar: Allee Can Viceroy of the Bullochies, and lieth in the City of Buckera: Sawber Can Viceroy of the Multans, and Can Bullard Viceroy of the Indoſtands.

Theſe are the names of his ten Viceroys, being all Heathens, but very worthy men, and expert in the warres. Hee hath a great number of Noble men to attend on him. An Earle is called a Nawbob, and they are the chiefs men that attend on him, when he goeth

eth

eth abroad: for at home none attend him but Eunuches or gelded men.

His Lord chiefe Justice is an Eunuch, and is called Awlee Nawbob: hee is thought to bee woorth twenty English millions: Hee keepeth twenty Elephants, one hundreth and fifty Camels and Dromedaries, and fiue hundreth Horse to attend on him.

The Lord Treasurer is a mighty man, called Sultan Carowdon: Hee hath forty Elephants to attend him, two hundred Camels and Dromedaries, and one thousand Horse at his seruice. And when he commeth to sit in his place of Justice, hee is brought vpon an Elephant clad in cloth of gold or siluer, and sometimes in a Pollankan, carried by foure slaues, he lying in it, as if hee lay in a cradle, in as great pomp and ease as may bee, and hath foure maces of siluer and gilt carried before him, and ten banners, and as great attendance, as if hee were a King; yet on Twesdaies and Thursdaies the King himselfe sits in Judgement of all causes: He custometh all strangers goods himselfe, the custome being but small at his pleasure, as sometimes, the value of ten shillings, custometh goods woorth two hundreth pound. Also if a Merchant stranger bring wares or merchandize from a farre Countrey: as from Chyna, Bengalla, and thinketh hee shall make a bad voiage, or lose thereby: if hee acquaint the King therewith, and that the Merchandize bee fit for Kings, Princes and Noble men, the King himselfe will take part thereof, and cause his Nobles to take the rest, at such rates as the Merchant shall not only bee a sauer, but a great gainer thereby.

The Mogoll lyueth in as great state and pomp as may be deuised both for Maiestie and princely pleasure; for hee had brought before him euery day during our aboude there, 50. Elephants royall. clad in cloth of gold and siluer, with drums, fifes and trumpets, whereof, some fight one with another, wounding one another vs-

ry

ry deadly, and cannot be parted but with Rackets of wilde fier, made round like hoopes, & so ran the some in their faces: and some of them fight with wilde horses, as one Elephant with 6 horses, whereof he hath killed 3. instantly by clasping his trunk about their neckes, and so pulling them to him, with his teeth break.th their necks.

Also there are tame Elephants, that will take the viceroyes sonnes being the Kings pages, with their trunks, gaping as they would eat them, and yet verie gently will set them vpon his owne head, and hauing sitten there a good space, will set them downe againe on their feet as tenderly as a mother would set downe her owne childe, doing them no harme at all.

The Elephant will not goe out of the sight of his female, nor will he be ruled if he doe: this I can speake by experience, hauing seene triall made thereof. Also euery he Elephant hath 3. or 4. females, & I saw one that had 4. females and 12 young ones of his owne begetting.

Their ingendring together is strange, for the female lieth downe on her back, and he commeth vpon her, and so ingender. But if he perceiue any man to behold or see him thus ingendring, hee will kill him if he can.

Also the King hath Deare, Rammes, Wraathoes or Beazors, Lyons, Leopards, and Wolues, that fight before him. Also if a Caualier be condemned for any offence & iudged to die, he may by the custom of the Countrey, craue combate with a Lion for his life, (which the King denieth to none that craue it) as for example, I saw one that at the first incounter stroke the Lion with his fist that he felled him, but the Lion recouering returned with great furie and violence, and caught such hold on him, that he rent out his guts, with the heart and liuer, and so tore him in peeces: and this was performed before the King.

Also there are horses that fight with Allegators or Crocodiles in Tancks or ponds of water, where I also

saw

faw one Allegator kil ·. foure horfes at one time. There
is alfo a faire Riuer called Indawe, running from thence
to Mefopotamia, & carrieth boats or lighters of 40. tun,
and is replenifhed with fifh of all forts.

Alfo there are 4. Bafars or markets every day in the
weeke, and great ftore of all things to be bought & fold
there, and at a very reafonable rate. As a hen for 1. pence,
a Turkey for 6. pence, a liue hare for 2. a dollar, a fheep for
2. fhillings, a goat for 2. fhillings, a couple of oxen for 4.
dollars, being 16. fhillings fterling, a good hogge for 2.
fhillings, but none buy them but Chriftians, and none
fell them but the Bannians, who bree them, and as much
fifh for 3. pence, as will ferue 5. reafonable men at a
meale.

Alfo great ftore of fruit, as Limmons, Oranges, Apri-
cockes, Grapes, Peares, Apples and Plummes; But
with their Grapes they make no wines, becaufe their
lawes forbid it : Alfo Raifins as great and faire as
Raifins of Damafco, with great ftore of cloth of gold,
veluets and filkes out of Perfia, and filkes and cloth of
gold from Chyna: but thofe are courfe and low prifed ;
but abundance are there vended: and Captaine Hawkins thinketh that our Richer filkes, veluets, and fuch
like would be excellent good commodities there.

But efpecially our Cloth of light coloures. For there
is no Cloth, but a kind of courfe Cloth like Cotton, w
is made at Lyhore, and at a Towne called Efmeere:
and their fineft & beft, is a kind of courfe red cloth, like
a Ven ce red, & this is the vfuall wearing for the chief-
eft Caualiers; & thefe are all the places of cloathing that
I could by any meanes heare of in all that Country.

The word Mogol in their language is as much as to
fay, the great white King; for he is a white man and of
the Race of the Tartares. Hee is King of many kingdomes, & walketh himfelfe in his ftile, Patte fhaw Shelham Shogh, that is, the King of all the great coynes. For
there is a feuerall coyne at Lahore, another at Brampott,

another

another at Surrot, another at Cambaia, another at Sab-
barton, and another at Awgrn : And for his seuerall
Ringdomes, he is King of the Guzarats, of the Bannians, of the Bullotts of Callicot and Bengoila which are
Gentiles, of the Indestands of the Mogolles, of the Hen-
douns, of the Moltans, of the Puttans, of the Bullochies,
and of the Alkeysors, with some other, which I cannot
particularly nane. Also he wziteth himselfe the r.ynth
King from Tamberlaine. And to this his great Citc he is
also of as great power, wealth and command, yet will
he bzgenone of what Nationsoeuer to forsake their Re-
ligions, but essermeth any man somuch the better, by
howrmuch the moze he is firme and constant in his Religion, e of all other he maketh most accompt of Chzi-
stians, and will allow them double the meanes that hee
glaeth to any othernation, and keepeth continvally two
Chzistian Friers, to conuerse with them in ye Chziskti-
an Religion and manners of Chzistendome. He hath
also the picture of our Lady in the place of his pzater oz
Religious pzoceedings, and hath oftentimes sald, that
he could find in his heart to be a Chzistian, if they had
not so many Gods : There was at my being there an
Armenian Chzistian, that in hope of gaine and pzeferment turned Moze, which being told the King, hee said,
If he thought to saue his soule thereby, that was a sufficient Recompence for him, but he would rather haue
giuen him pzeferment if he had kept himselfe still a
Chzistian.

The Mogoll is also verie bountifull, for to one that
gaue him a little deere, he gaue 1000 Ruckees, being
100. pound sterling: also to another that gaue him a couple of land Spanniels, he gaue the like reward, eto another that gaue him two Cocks he gaue 2000 Ruckees.

Also there be excellent faire Hawkes of all sozts from
the Goshauke to the Spar-hauke, and great nore of
game, as Phesants, Partridges, Plouers, Quailes,
Mailard, and of all other sozts of fowles in great plentie.
                                                  There

There are no great Dogges but a kind of Mungrels, whereof two will hardly kill a Deere in a whole day, and yet they are so choise ouer them, that they make them coates to keepe them warme and cleane. Nor haue they any Parkes, but Forrests, and Commons, wherein any man may hunt that will, saue only within 5. miles of Agra, roundabout which is lymited and reserued for the Kings priuate pleasure onely.

The King hath there begun a goodly monument for his Father, which hath been already 9. yeeres in building, and will hardly be finished in 5. yeeres more, and yet there are continually 5000. workemen at worke thereon.

The substance therof, is very fine marble, curiously wrought.

It is in forme 9. square, being 2. English miles about and 9. stories in height.

Also, it was credibly reported vnto me by a Christian Frier (who solemnly protested he heard the king him selfe speake it) that hee intended to bestow a hundreth millions of Treasure on that monument.

And hauing viewed and seene this great and rich Citie of Agra with the pleasures and Commodities thereof; on the 18. day of Ianuarie, my selfe with Ioseph Salbancke and Iohn Frencham, went to the King and craued his Passe for England, who very courteously demanded of vs, if we would serue him in his wars, offering vs what maintenance we would aske of him; which wee humbly excused, both in regard of this our voiage, wherein diuers others besides our selues, were partners, as also, in regard we had Wiues and Children in our owne Countrie, to whom both by Law and Nature, wee were bound to make returne, if it were possible; whereupon most graciously he granted vs his Passe, vnder his hand & great Seale, for our safe conduct thorow all his Kingdomes and Dominions. Then his chiefe Secretary went with vs to his third Queene (for it is said that hee

hath ten Quæenes, one thousand Concubines, and two
hundzeth Eunuches.) And this Quæene is kæper of his
great Seale, where it was sealed and deliuered vnto vs.
Then I also went to the chiefe Frier, and craued his letters, as well to the kings and Pzinces, whose kingdoms
and Dominions we were to passe thozow, as also to the
Clergy and places of Religion, which he most willingly
granted, bæing a man of great credit there, and greatly
estæmed and well knowne in other kingdomes.

Also he gaue me his letters of commendations to one
Iohn Midnall an English Merchant oz Factoz, who had
lien in Agra thzæe yæeres: but befoze I came into England, Iohn Midnall was gone againe foz the East Indies,
and I deliuered his letter to Mr *GREEN AWAY*, De-
puty gouernoz in London foz the Company of the East
Indian Merchants.

The one and twentieth day , wee tooke our leaue of
Captaine Hawkins, whom wee left there in great credit
with the king , bæing allowed one hundzeth Ruckæs a
day, which is ten pound sterling, and is intituled by the
name of a Can, which is a knight, and kæpeth company
with the greatest Noblemen belonging to the king: and
hee sæmeth very willing to doe his Country good. And
this is as much as I can say concerning him.

The 21. day we tooke our iourney towards England,
being 5. English men, viz. my selfe, Ioseph Salebancke ,
Iohn Frencham, Richard Martin, and Richard Fox, and
Guilliam Ashlee a Moze our guide, and trauelled towards Isphan in Persia, and so with 5. hozses and 2. Camels, we tooke the way to Biany, because Iohn Midnall
had gone the way by Lahor befoze, also this way was
but two moneths iourney, though very dangerous, and
that by Lahor was 4. moneths iourney and without danger, viz.

From Agra we came to Fetterbarre being 12. course.
And fró thence to Bianic, being 11. course moze. And this
is the chiefest place foz Indico in all the East Indies,
                                                      where

where are 12. Indico Milles.

The Indico groweth in small bushes like gooseberry bushes, and carrieth a seede like Cabbege seed. And being cut downe, is laid on heapes for halfa yeere to rot, and then brought into a vault to be troden with Oxen, to tread the Indico from the stalkes, and so to the Milles to be ground very fine: and lastly, is boiled in Furnaces, and very well refined and sorted into seuerall sorts.

A seere of Indico in Biany is worth ten pence, which seere doth containe twenty ounces at the least. This I know to be true, and brought a sample of the Indico home with mee. And for this Indico & the Anneele that is made thereof, there is much trading of Merchants from Agra and Lohore.

The 25. day, we came to Hendowne, being twenty fiue course, this is an ancient faire City, where is also good store of course Indico.

The 26. day, we came to Mogoll being 14. course. This is a small market Towne, where are also course Indico and Callicoes.

The 27. day we went some 12. course to a small Village called Halitor.

The 28. day, we trauelled 12. course to a small Village called Chatsoe, where are sheepe and goats great store, and very cheape.

The 29. day, we went 12. course to a small Town called Laddanna, and there are great store of Cotten Wools.

The 30. day, we went eight course to a small town called Mosabad, where is great store of corne.

The 31. day we went 14. course to Bandason a small Village

The first day of Februarp we came to a faire Riuer called Paddar, that runneth to Guzarat, and this Riuer parteth the Dominions of the Indestands and Hendownes, and falleth into the gulph of Persia. And from thence we went to the City of Esmeere, being twelue course from Bandaſon.

Here the great Mogol hath a ſtately houſe, where are continually kept 600. Elephants, and 1000. Horſes for the warres, to bee ready at the Kings command.

There is great ſtore of wools, and much cloathing for coorſe cloth and cottens, alſo Iauelins, Bowes and Arrowes, Armour, Swords, and other weapons for the Warres, and two Baſars or Markets euery weeke.

The Indeſtands are very gallant people, and great Merchants into moſt parts of the world.

The ſecond day, wee went into the Hendownes Countrey, ſome 12. courſe, and came to Richmall, where is great ſtore of Game, and a pleaſant place for hawking and hunting.

The fourth day, we went 12. courſe, to Mearta, a faire City, where I ſaw three faire and ancient Tombes or Monuments of the Hendownes, there are three Baſars or Markets euery weeke. Alſo great ſtore of Indico, cotten wooll, yarne, and cloth.

This City in my iudgement is as big as the City of Exceter.

The ſixth day wee went ſome twelue courſe to Hurſallo, a ſmall Village.

The ſeuenth day we went 14. courſe to Lauara, a ſmall village, where is great ſtore of Corne, Cattell, and Sheepe and very good cheape.

The eight day, we went 12. courſe to Towry, a Towne of Garriſon of the Hendownes.

The ninth day, we went 11. courſe to Chummo a ſmall Village.

The tenth day, we went 13. courſe to Moulto a Village.

The 11. day, we went 10. courſe to Pucker a ſmall Village.

The

The 12. day, we went 12. courſe to Senawra a little Towne.

The 13. day, we went but fiue courſe to Baſonpee a ſmall village.

The 14. day, we went fiue courſe moze to Giſſemceere, a faire City, and hath in it a ſtrong Caſtle, where lyeth a grand Cauilier. Alſo there is great trading of Merchandize by Land, and in the Caſtle are thirty peeces of Ozdnance.

The 18. day, we went from thence ſome 14. courſo ouer the ſands, that part the Hendownes and Multans, and lay in the fields.

The Hendownes are naturally deſtended from the Gentiles, yet refuſe no manner of meat, fleſh, noz fiſh, and are many of them very notable theeues. They pzay naked, dzeſſe and eat their meat naked, and where they dzeſſe and eat their meat, they make a circle, within which circle none muſt enter, during the time of their dzeſſing and eating their meat.

Their women are bzought vp of childzen with ſhackles, ſome of ſiluer, ſome of bzaſſe, and ſome of Iron on their legs, and rings in their eares, all which are ſtill increaſed oz made bigger, as they grow in yeres and bigneſſe, ſo that in time they haue holes in their eares ſo great that a man may thzuſt his finger thozow. Alſo they doe weare bzacelets of Elephants teeth about their armes from the wziſt to the elbow.

The 19. day, wee went eight courſo and lay in the Fields.

The 20. day, wee went 12. courſe moze, and lay in the fields.

The twenty one day, we went 12. courſe and lay by a well ſome 60. fathome deepe, where water was very ſcarſe.

The 22 day, we trauelled 16. courſe, where wee could get no better water then was almoſt halfe Cowpiſſe.

The 23. day we went some 15. course, and lay in the fields.

The 24 day, wee went some fiue course, and came to three Townes, viz. Roree, Buckar, and Sucker, where is a gallant fresh Riuer, and small ships that may goe to Armoose, as the Townsmen report. Now the shipping belongeth to Roree, being some fifty or sixty saile, and of the burden of fourty, fifty, and sixty tun, whereby there is trade of Merchandize as far as the coast of Molindee, and as far as Mosembique, and this Riuer falleth into the gulph of Persia.

Buckar standeth in the middle of the Riuer, which maketh it in forme of an Iland, and is besides very strongly built.

The Indians cal this Riuer, the Riuer of Damiadee. And in this Towne of Buckar, lieth Allee Can the Mogols Viceroy of the Bullochies, who are such a stubborne & rebellious people, that hee keepeth that strong hold of purpose to retire vnto, and to gather a head, and renew his forces at all assaies, to subdue and keepe them in awe and obedience, which notwithstanding he can hardly doe. Also this Allee Can is a very worthy and bountifull Prince, who gaue vs very gallant and kinde entertainment, and commanded vs to come dayly to his Court, where wee had both costly and plentifull diet at all times, and heere wee left Io. Frencham (one of our company) sicke.

Sucker is a Towne consisting most of Weauers and Diers, and liue by cloathing, and serue the Countrey round about, and this is the first Towne of the Bullochies. And Roree the last confins towne of the Multans, who are good husbandmen and painefull people, and deale much in Merchandize, as Cloth, Indico, and other commodities, and are very good people to deale withall, yet their Religion is Mahometicall.

At Sucker wee stayd 24. dayes and more for a Coffilo or Conuoy: For the Captaine of the Castle would

not

not suffer vs to goe without one, because the way was dangerous and full of Thæues, which afterwards we found true; for had we not (by the great prouidence of God) escaped their hands, it had cost vs our liues, and yet it cost vs some money besides.

The 25. day of March, 1610, wée came from Sucker, and trauelled ouer the plaines some thrée course or thereabouts.

The 26. day wee trauelled thorow the woods or Desarts some thrée course more.

The 27. day, wée went thrée course more thorow the Desarts, and there wée tooke in water for two daies, which was but bad water neither, but there was no better to be had, nor any towne to come to, vntill we came to Gorra, some eight course distant from thence, which was on the 28. day at night, where wée rested two daies, and were very well vsed, yet being a Towne of the Bullochies and Rebels, wée were in great feare, but wee found no such cause, God be praysed.

The Bullochies are Men-eaters, being men of huge limmes and proportion, euen giantlike, nor are they of any Religion at all, saue only that they worship the Sunne.

The 21. day, we came to Norry, being about 10. course, and this is the last Towne of the Bullochies; and so to the Puttans.

The first day of Aprill, we tooke our iourney ouer the plaines early in the morning, and about breake of day wee met with tenne or twelue men playing on fiddles, as if they had come in friendly maner to welcome vs, but indéed they were no better then Thæues that intended to rob and pillage vs, for by the Sun-rising wee were beset round with them and their companions, whose certaine number wee could not discerne nor know.

And though wée had a Caffeloe or Conuoy of two
hundred

hundred strong, yet wee were glad to intreat the Captaines of that vnruly Crew to stand our friend, and
both to bribe him priuatly, and to pay openly besides
in the name of a custom, twenty Chekanees in gold,
nor would all this haue serued the turne, but for the
Mogols Passe vnder his hand and great seale, which
they much feared, but that all our throats had bene
cut, as other in greater number had formerly bene;
yet at last vpon this friendly composition, they gar-
ded and conducted vs thorow their Countrey, vntill wee were past all danger, and so departed, and
that day wee trauelled some nine course ouer the
plaines, and tooke vp our lodging in the plaine
fields.

The second day wee trauelled some eight course to
a Towne called Dudder, where wee rested two
daies.

The fifth day, we trauelled eight course ouer the
mountaines.

The sixth day, we went ten course ouer the mountaines.

The seuenth day, we went eight course ouer the
Mountaines,

The eight day, we went eight course to Vachesto,
a Towne of ciuill and quiet Gouernment, where wee
rested that night.

The ninth day we went three or foure course ouer the
mountaines, and lay in the fields.

The tenth day we went some eight course in the
mountaines.

The eleuenth day, we went nine or ten course in the
Mountaines.

The twelfth day we went some nine or ten course in
the mountaines.

The thirteenth day we went nine or ten course in
the mountaines.

The fourteenth day we went some fourteene course
ouer

The 15. day we came to Candahar, being but two courſe from thence, where wee ſtaied 10. or 11. daies.

This is a great and gallant Citie of the Puttans, where Swadder Conuiceroy of the Puttans keepeth his Court and reſidence.

There is great and continuall traffique by land, from Perſia, Indeſtand, Meſopotamia, and from all partes betweene that and China, with all ſortes of merchandize and commodities which thoſe Countries yeeld ; For there are continually 7. or 8. thouſand Camels about the Citie, which trade to and fro with merchandize.

Alſo the viceroy hath continually 40000. horſe for the warres in readineſſe for feare of Rebellion, becauſe the Puttans are a ſtrong and warlike people, and inclined to rebellion, by reaſon they came vnder the Mogols gouernment and ſubiection by force and conqueſt, and therefore loue him not in their hearts, but obey him for feare.

The 6. day of May we tooke our iourney for Iſpahawne in Perſia, and trauelled ſome 8 courſe that day, and came to a gallant Riuer, where were two Townes, on each ſide of the Riuer one, and at one of theſe Towne called Langor, we reſted that night.

The 7. day we went ſome 6. or 7. courſe ouer the plaines.

The 8. day we went in like manner ſome 7. courſe more, and lay in the fields.

The 9. day we went ouer the plaines ſome 12. courſe, and came to a great Riuer, which diuideth the land of the Puttans from Perſia, and there we paid cuſtome for our Owts or Camels, and reſted 2. daies by the Riuer ſide.

The 11. day we were ferried ouer the Riuer, which is called Sabbaa, to a caſtle a courſe from thence, and neer to a Towne called Grees.

This Riuer diuideth the confines of the great Mogoll and the King.

The Puttans are a warlike and goodly people, and weare

their

their beards long, which the Mogols doe hate, also they
worship the great God of heauen, and despise Mahomet.

Their Priests goe in Sackcloth with great Chaines
about their middles ; And doe fall downe and pray continually in Sackcloth and Ashes.

Grees the
first Towne
of Persia.

And so passing out of the great Mogols kingdomes
and dominions, we came to the Towne of Grees being
the first Towne of Persia, where we rested a day and a
night.

The Towne of Grees, is a frontier Towne, and
therefore the King or (as they call him) the Shawbash of
Persia keepeth heere a garrison of ten thousand men,
and a gouernour to command them.

The 14. day we went ouer the plaines 6. forsongs:
euery forsong being a league, and euery league 2. course,
and rested in the fields.

The 15. day we trauelled ouer the plaines some 6. forsongs more, and came to a Castle, where we refreshed our
selues and our cattel, and there we rested our selues two
dayes to stay for a Coffeloe or conuoy which came to vs
the 14. day at night.

The 18. day we went 5. forsongs ouer the fields or
plaines, and lay in the fields.

The 19. day at night we trauelled some 4. forsongs to
a Towne called Doctorcham, where wee stayed all the
next day and night.

The 21. day we trauelled some 5. or 6. forsongs in the
night to a Towne called Sehawe, and thus for certaine
dayes wee trauelled all by night, by reason of the extreme
heat in the day time.

The 22. day at night wee trauelled some 6. forsongs
ouer the plaines.

The 23. day at night we went 5. forsongs to a Town
called Vea, where are great store of Feltmakers, which also make felt Carpets, & weauers of Turkie Carpets: there
are also great store of Dates, and all sorts of fruits.

The 24. day wee trauelled some 6. forsongs to a faire
Citie

Citie called Parra, where we ſtaied 22. daies for a Coffeloe or Connoy, my ſelfe being alſo ſicke there : there is
great trading of merchandize, and great ſtore of raw ſilke,
which in the Perſian tongue is called Aueriſham.

The 6. day we went ſome 2. forſongs ouer the mountaines.

The 7. day we went 4. or 5. forſongs ouer the mountaines.

The 8. day we went 7. forſongs.

The 9. day we went ſome 5. forſongs.

The 10. day we went 10. forſongs all in the mountaines.

The 11. day we trauelled ſome 3. forſongs to a towne
called Banda, being but a harbor or lodging place.

The 12. day wée went ſome 3. forſongs ouer the
plaines.

The 13. day we trauelled ſome 5. forſongs ouer the
plaines, and reſted till the 14. day at night, and then trauelled ſome 7. forſongs and a halfe.

The 15. day wee came to a Towne called Sunday,
where we reſted that night and all the next day and
night.

The 17. day we trauelled ſome 7. forſongs and a halfe
ouer the plaines.

The 18. day wée went in like manner ſome 9. forſongs.

The 19. day we went 5. forſongs to a Towne called
Bcaſta.

The 20. day we went ſome 4. forſongs.

The 21. day we trauelled ſome 6. forſongs to a towne
called Guſta, where we reſted a day and a night.

The 23. day we trauelled 4. forſongs to a watering
place.

The 24. day we trauelled 10. forſongs, and reſted in
the fields,

The 25. day we trauelled 7. forſongs to a Towne called Dattee, where was great ſtore of Muſkmillions, and

there

there we had good releafe.

The 26. day we travelled some 4. forsongs, to a place where was a gallant vawlt with water.

The 27. day we went some 7. forsongs, to a Towne called Yesday.

The 28. day we went some 5. forsongs, to a Towne called Pahanauens, where we rested 2. daies and two nights.

There is great store of raw silke, or Auerisham as they call it.

The 2. day of Iuly we went 5. forsongs ouer the plaines.

The third day we went 8. forsongs ouer the barren and wilde plaines, where we had no water but salt water, and the ground all couered ouer with salt.

The 4. day we trauelled 7. forsongs in salt ground, and none but salt water.

The 5. day we went 15. forsongs for want of water in a most barren and dry Country, and came to a town called Bibe, where we rested two daies and two nights.

The 8. day we trauelled some 14. forsongs to a Towne called Godanna: where we rested that night and the next day and night, and here is also great store of raw silke.

The 10. day we trauelled some 10 forsongs to a Towne called Hemda, where are great store of Grapes and Muskmillions.

The 12. day we trauelled some 15. forsongs to a Towne called Carneta.

The 13. day we went 6. or 7. forsongs to a Towne called Orrinkca, a lodging Towne.

The 14. day we went but 4. forsongs to a little village.

The 15. day we went 5. forsongs to a Towne called Gowra, being a faire great Towne, where is great store of raw silkes, bed couerings, silke carpets, cotten

Carpets,

Carpets, and such like commodities ; and there wee ſtaied that night , and the next day and night.

The ſeuenteenth day , we went nine foꝛſongs, befoꝛe we could finde any water.

The eightœnth day , we trauelled fiue foꝛſongs to a little Uillage.

The nineteenth day , we went ſeuen foꝛſongs ouer the plaines.

The twentieth day , wee went ſome fiue foꝛſongs ouer the plaines.

The twenty one day , wée trauelled ſome fiue foꝛſongs ouer the plaines.

The twenty two day , we went two foꝛſongs and a halfe.

The twenty thꝛée day , we came to Iſpahawne.

The twenty fourth day , we entred into the City, where wée ſtaid eleuen oꝛ twelue daies.

This City of Iſpahawne, is a gallant City, and one of the pꝛincipall Cities of Perſia , and aboundeth in traffique of all ſoꝛts of Merchandiſe. There are many great Surroies, where are houſes made of purpoſe foꝛ the laying in and kéeping of Merchants goods, and to harbour and lodge themſelues and their Camels, Hoꝛſes oꝛ other Cattel, and pꝛouiſion ; the pꝛofits of which Surroies redound to the King onely.

The whole Countrey aboue a hundꝛed miles round about , doe wholly and generally trade to this City, with their chiefeſt and beſt commodities. There is alſo a place in foꝛme like the Exchange, of an ineſtimable wealth, where is nothing to be ſold but things of great value and woꝛth : As Cloth of gold, ſiluer and tiſſue, ſattins, veluets, Iewels and pearles. In one end are nothing but raw ſilkes : in another end are twiſted and wꝛought ſilkes : In another none but Merchant-tailoꝛs, who ſell all ſoꝛts of apparell ready made, as it is in Birching lane, but farre moꝛe rich, and all of the Perſian faſhion, as ſutes of cloth of gold,

and

and ſiluer, veluet, ſatten, taffety, Callico, and noue almoſt of any wozſer ſozts.

Alſo there is great ſtoze of Indico and Annále, and of all manner of Dzugs, which are ſold by Iewes and other ſtrangers that ſend them thither, and haue continuall trading there.

Alſo there are Cammels, the beſt and ſtrongeſt that are to bée ſound, with gallant Hozſes aud Mules a-bundance. Foz whereas an ozdinary Camels load is ſiue hundzed waight, the Perſian Cammels load is vſu-ally 800. waight.

The Shawbaſh (oz, as we call him, the King) hath there diuers gallant and ſtately houſes, and banque-ting houſes, with Ozchards, Gardens, Spzings, ponds of water, walks and Galleries, as pleaſantly ſeated and artificially contriued, as can be thought oz deuiſed. But the King him ſelfe befoze my comming thither, was remoued to a place called Tobrin, as it was told me by the Chziſtian Friers.

And at his chiefeſt houſe ſtanding ouer againſt the great Baſar oz Market place, there are good ſtoze of bzaſſe Ozdnance ozderly planted befoze the gate thereof, foz defence, if néede be, as namely, two Demy Cannons, two whole Culuerings, two Cannon Pe-dzars, and thirty other field Péces.

Alſo hére I made enquiry of Maſter Robert Sher-ley, thinking to haue had ſome aſſiſtance, and better directions from him, oz by his pzocurement, in my Iourney, but it was tolo me directly that hé was de-parted ſome ſeuen months befoze foz England, and had his way by the Caſpian Seas, being two months Iour-ney from Iſpahawn: That is to ſay, himſelfe, and his wife, being a woman of great wozth and eſtéeme in that Country, with Camels and Hozſes to carry his treaſure, ſtuffe, and pzouiſion, and many attendants both men and women. And in his Company, one Captaine   and ſixe oz ſeuen Engliſhmen moze.

Alſo

Also there are great store of Grapes and Wines, and of all sorts of fruits ; their stronger Wines like vnto Canary Sacks, their red Wines like high Counttrey Claret, and their smaller Wines like to Iland Wines. Also victuals good store and good cheape.

And there lieth continually a Portugall Embassador, and fiue Portugall Friers , who haue a Church, and a house to entertaine Roman Catholiks , and other Chꝛistians at their pleasures, and haue meanes sufficient to maintaine the same.

A Portugal Embassador Leigier.

Also there are great store of Armenian Chꝛistians, and some Greekes , who line all at free liberty, without restraint or controll for their Religion. And so much for the great and rich City of Ispahawne.

The sixth day of August, wee departed from thence, and trauelled some sixe forsongs , and lay in the fields close by a riuer side.

The seuenth day, we trauelled ten forsongs in the Desarts, and on the eight day sixe forsongs moꝛe to the Towne of Coꝛꝛonday.

The ninth day to Miskerion, and so directly to Bugdad, or Babylon, being a months Journey : that is to say, sixe forsongs to Miskerion.

The tenth day, wee went ten forsongs in the Desarts.

The eleuenth day, eleuen forsongs in the Desarts.

The twelfe day, nine forsongs moꝛe in the Desarts.

The thirteenth day, wee went fourteene forsongs to a little Village called Corryn.

The fourteenth day, ten forsongs in the Desarts.

The fifteenth day, nine forsongs in the Desarts.

The sixteenth day, we trauelled nine or ten forsongs to a little Towne called Lackercee.

The seuenteenth day wee trauelled eight forsongs in the Desarts.

The eighteenth day, we trauelled twelue forsongs

in the Desarts to a water-Mill, where we lay all night.

The nintænth day, wée went fourtéene forsongs thorow the Desarts, to a little Towne called Corber.

The twentieth day, we trauelled twelue forsongs, to a Cloth towne: that is to say, where all the houses were made of hairy cloth like tents, and there wee rested two daies.

The thré and twentieth day, we trauelled some eight forsongs in the Desarts.

The foure and twentieth day, wée trauelled some nine or tenne forsongs ouer the Desarts, to another Cloth towne.

The twentie fiue day, wée went thorow a mighty great Wood, being fiftéene forsongs in length, where we went downe such an extreme stéepe hill, that wée broke two of our Camels necks, and had much to doe to goe downe the same our selues without harme, and there we rested allnight.

The fire and twentieth day, wée went some two forsongs to another Cloth towne, where wee rested thrée daies and thrée nights, and there we paid Custome for our Camels to a great City, being but a forsong from thence, and is called Nezzeret, where, on the top of a mighty great mountaine, was a monument of a great Sultan, or Gentleman: and when we asked, Why he was buried there? it was directly answered, Because he was so much the neerer to heauen.

The thirtieth day, we trauelled ten forsongs to the Riuer of Synnee, which runneth into the Riuer Euphrates, and deuideth the confines of Persia and Arabia, and by the Riuer side were remaining some old walles of a ruinated Towne of Persia, which were rayet and destroied by the Turkes and Arabians.

The one and thirtieth day, we trauelled eight forsongs in a waste Countrey, where we lay by a Well all night.

Among

Amongſt the Perſians, the Sultans or Gentlemen, and men of better ſort, are gallant men, and of ciuill and courteous behauiour : but the baſer ſort, are ſullen, vnciuill, and men of very bad conditions. And generally they doo woꝛſhip Mahomet, and are common Buggerers, as the Turks are, yet they are people that labour extremely, as in digging, planting, and ſowing, and in picking of Cotten wooll, and other wooll, in ſpinning and making Coats, and other things of felt. Noꝛ haue they almoſt any raine there, but by extreme labour let the water out of the Riuers, into their Paſtures and Coꝛne grounds.

There are good ſhæpe and goats plenty, but Kine and Oxen are very ſcarce. Alſo Turkies and Hennes and other ſoꝛts of fowles plenty.

And there a man may trauell without danger of robbing, foꝛ it is there a ſtrange thing to heare of a thæfe. And ſomuch foꝛ Perſia, and the Perſians.

The firſt day of September, wæ trauelled twelue foꝛſongs to a great Towne called Sabbercam, being the firſt towne that wæ came to in Arabia, where are growing great ſtoꝛe of Pomegranats, which the Arabians doe call Anarres. This is a Towne of Garriſon of the Arabians, and hære wæ ſtaied a day and a night.

The third day, we trauelled fouretæne foꝛſongs to a towne called Buldad, where we alſo pald cuſtome, and hære wæ ſtaied a day and a night. This is alſo a towne of Garriſon and full of thæues, and at our comming out of the towne, Ioſeph Salebancke one of my Companions, ſtaying but a little behind the Coffeloe oꝛ Connoy, was by the Arabians robbed, ſtripped and extremely beaten and hurt. So that if by chance I had not reſerued ſome 100. Chickænoes, wæ had then bæne both quite deſtitute of money to bꝛing vs home into our Countrey.

The ſixth day wæ trauelled eightæne foꝛſongs to the great City of Bagdet, oꝛ Babylon, where wee ſtaied

I   vntill

vntill the twentie two day of October following.

This City standeth vpon the great Riuer Euphrates, and is a great, rich, and strong City, with mighty strong wals, whereon are planted 100. and twenty péeces of brasse Ordnance.

Also there are ships small and great to the number of 300. saile, belonging to this Citie, and great trade of Merchandize both by water and land.

It is not past 4. yéeres since the Turke wan this City from the Persians.

Also there is a floting bridge built vpon 33. great lighters strongly chained and fastened together, from Bugdad ouer Euphrates, to olde Babylon standing ouer against Bugdad on the other side of the Riuer. And within a league from thence standeth the Remainder of the Ruynated Tower of Babel, being one of the wonders of the world.

In Bugdad, lieth one of the Turkes grand Bashawes, called by the name of Mahomet Patteshogh, who is e-stéemed as a Viceroy, and is gouernor of the City vn-der the great Turke.

There are only two Venetian factors, who trade for inestimable wealth in Merchandize of all sorts. Also some small number of Armenians, which are all the Christians that are there resident.

The Turke is a valiant and resolute Souldier, as by their proceedings may appeare, both in winning the City of Bugdad, and another City of as great strength as that, called Towras, and belonged also to the Persi-an, whereof the Mahomet Patteshogh had certaine in-telligence on the 12. day of October whilest wee were there.

And that the great Turke, or (as they call him) the Grand Gushell Bashe hassuredly thinketh and intendeth, in short space to approach to the wals of Ispahawne, be-ing a great and gallant Citie, and standeth farre with-in the kingdome of Persia.

The.

The 10. day of October there came vnto vs an Eng-
lith man called Iohn White, who said hee was sent for a
difcouery to the Eaft Indies, and was bound for Ifpa-
hawne to meet with Iohn Midnall, who vs affured him
not to be there, but at Armoofe.

Then did I and Iofeph Salebanke perfwade him
to trauell to the red fea or Cambaia, whether hee told
vs, Sir Henry Middleton was bound from England
with a good fhip called the Trades Increafe, of the burden of 1000. or 1100. tun, with another fhip called the
Cloue, and a Pinnis called the Pepper Corne, and the
caufe, why wee thus aduifed him was, for that hee, hauing the Turkifh language, might accompany my
friend Iofeph Salebancke to Sir Henry Middleton, to
acquaint him with the true difcourfe of our whole
voyage and trauels, whereby hee might beware of and
auoid the like dangers that wee fuftained and were in:
As alfo how and where to take his beft opportunity for
his lading, as time and occafion fhould ferue.

And vpon the 18. day Iofeph Salebancke and Iohn
White tooke their iourney accordingly, to a great City
called Balfara ftanding vpon the Riuer Euphrates, and
is 18. daies iourney from Bugdad, or Babylon, where
they were to meet with a Carrauant or conuoy, to conduct them to the Citie of Iudaia neere vnto the Red
Sea.

And although Iofeph Salebancke was then verie
poore, (hauing ben formerly robbed) yet was hee very
willing to take this long and dangerous iourney vpon
him for the good of his Country.

And all the good that I could doe for him, was to
procure him a Camell, and to lend him fome part of
my fmall ftore, being in all not about 6. pound fterling,
and fo I left them to the protection of the Almighty.

The 22. day of October wee tooke our iourney from
Bugdad or Babylon, to the City of Aleppo. And hauing
trauelled 60. leagues at the leaft, all thorow the de-

farts,

farts, which wee did in some 8. daies, wee came to a
Towne called Mussaw Cosam.

The 31. day we trauelled some 4. daies iourny thorow the desarts, to the Towne of Ruseele, being onely a thorow-faire or lodging place, & some 30. leagues
from Mussaw Cosam.

The 4. day of Nouember, we trauelled some eight
leagues to a small village called Deesh.

The 5. day wee set forwards towards Mussell, otherwise called Niniuy, being some 30. leagues or more
from Deesh, and trauelled thither in 5. daies.

The Citie is now much ruinated, and yet the Remainder thereof is as spacious and great, as most Cities that I haue seene in all my Trauels : within the City is a great Bashaw or gouernour vnder the great
Turke.

Also without the City there standeth a faire & strong
Castle vpon the bankes of the Riuer Tygris, where is
also another Bashaw or gouernor for the Castle and
Suburbs of the Citie.

There is no trade of Merchandize in this City, but
it is only kept by the Turke as a Towne of Garrison:
yet there are Armenian Christians, who haue their
Churches and Friers, and doe freely vse their Religion without checke or comptroll.

Also there are yet remaining manie ancient monuments, which make relation and shew, that it hath
bene a City of great antiquity and famous memory :
and in this City we staied 4. daies.

The 14. day wee went 4. leagues to a Castle called
Nussebaw, and rested that night, and the next day wee
trauelled 12. leagues more, and at night came to Nussebaw, where the Prophet Ionas preached to all the
Countries round about ; and there remaineth his picture in stone (though much defaced by the warres) yet
it is kept and maintained by the Christians, whereof
there are many dispersed amongst the Turkes, euen
since

fince the deftruction oz ouerthzow of Niniue by the
Turkes: and are now called by the name of Curgees.

From thence wee trauelled fome 25. leagues in thzée
daies, and on the 18. day at night came to Hamadaine,
an ancient Towne of the Armenians ; but much ruinated by the Turkes. Here wee faw many ancient monuments, which fhewed that it had bin a Towne of great
antiquity and wozth, and at this Towne we ftaied one
day and a night.

The 20. day we tooke our iourney towards a Towne
called Goubba, being 25. leagues and 3. daies iourney,
and came thither the 22. day at night, where wee met
with a Conful of Venice, and 5. Venetians moze, trauel-
ling to Bugdad of Babylon, and there wee ftaied a day
and a night.

The 24. day wee trauelled towards the great City of
Vlfawe being 25. leagues, and 3. daies iourney, and
came thither the 26. day at night, and there all trauellers
pay great cuftome.

This is a mighty ftrong City, and a continuall Garrifon kept there by the Turke.

Nozcan any Carrauant oz Conuoy, oz any paffenger
bee fuffered to lodge within the City : But in the day
time they may come into it to the Baffart oz market, to
buy neceffaries and fo depart againe : and here we ftaied
5. daies.

The 2. day of December wee tooke our iourney to
Beere a great Towne vpon the Riuer Euphrates, being 3. daies iourney, and 25. leagues diftant, whither
wee came the fourth day at night, and ftaied there one
day.

This is alfo a ftrong Towne of Garrifon.

The 6. day wee were ferried ouer the Riuer and
went 2. daies iourney, being fome 15. leagues, to the
Towne of Lumman , and came thither on the 7. day at
night.

The 8. day wee trauelled 10. leagues to the City of

I 3   Aleppo,

Aleppo, and came thither that night, and by the way wee trauelled 2. leagues thorow the plaines, where was nothing but figs, or as I may termeit, a forest of fig trées, and another place of as great length, being all vine trées, full of grapes.

And being come to the great and worthy City of Aleppo, wée went to the English house, where I found Master Paul Pinder to be Consul, a very worthy Gentleman, and well deseruing a place of so great credit and estéeme, at whose hand wee found very courteous and kind entertainement; for at my comming to him I was destitute both of money and cloathes, and so was my companion Richard Martin.

But he reléeued vs, first with meate, drinke, and lodging during our abode there, being some twelue dayes: also hee furnisht vs with apparell, and at our departure, with money for our iourney.

Also there was one M. Spike, who was both kind and bountifull vnto vs. And so were all the rest of y English Merchants) whom I cannot particularly name) both kinde & courteous vnto vs, which was vnto vs a great refreshing and comfort in our iourney.

Aleppo is a City of wonderfull great trading, and as well knowne to England (or at least to our English Merchants) as Kingston vpon Thames. And thus much I can say more of it, that within foure dayes after our comming thether, there came aboue two thousand Camels, laden with Silkes, and of all sorts of Marchandize, all or most whereof I ouerwent in my trauells, being in seuerall Carauants, some from Mesopotamia, some from Agro, some from the Indians, and some from Persia, and so at other times continually they come from thence, and other places whence any trading can come by Land.

The one and twentieth day, I tooke my leaue of Master Paul Pinder, Master Spike and the rest of the Merchants, and tooke my iourney, (together with my

Companion

Companion Richard Martin) for Tripolie, and that day wee trauelled some seuen leagues ouer the Desarts, and rested two houres, and then trauelled some 15. leagues farther, to an old Towne called Asheewe, where wee rested halfe a day and baited, and then trauelled some ten leagues moze and baited, and rested our selues in the fields some foure houres, and then trauelled ten leagues moze to a Towne called Hamam. And the reason why wee trauelled thus hard, was to keepe company with a Carrauant oz Conuoy of 1000. strong, who were bound foz Mecha, where their great Mahomet was then resident: whereas else wee should haue trauelled in great danger and hazard of our liues, by reason the Countrey is so full of theeues.

In this Towne are many Weauers, that make great stoze of Dimatree, and schamatree, and Cottons: also it is a great thozow faire, and there is a great Ostrie oz Inne, which they call a Caan, and there wee rested two daies.

The sixe and twentieth day, we trauelled some eight leagues to a little Towne called Roma, where wee lay all night.

The seuen and twentieth day, wee trauelled some eight leagues moze to a Monastery called Huddreaslins, which was built by an Armenian Christian, who gaue sufficiet maintenance to pzouide Oliues, bzead, and Oile foz Lamps, foz the harbour and reliefe of all Christian trauellers : and there is the picture of Saint George on Horsebacke fighting with the Dzagon, and his picture on foot, and his Crosse, and mention in old Roman pzint of his noble and memozable acts, which Relique is much honozed by many Christians as they trauell by the same, and to that end there is a Chappell and Lampes burning therein continually.

The twenty eight day wee went some tenne leagues to a little Towne called Hone, and lay there that night.

The.

The 29. day, we travelled to Tripolis, being tenne leagues from thence, where wee found the good ship, the Great Exchange of London, whereof Master Robert Bradshawe of Ratliffe was both Captaine and Master; who not aboue ten daies before, was in great danger of shipwracke, breaking their Cables and Ancors, so that the ship droue and was in great distresse: So that they were faine to cut the maine Mast ouerboord, being within twice the ships length of the rocks, yet by Gods good prouidence, one Cable and Ancor held, and so both ship and men were saued, all the men hauing stripped themselues to saue their liues by swimming, or otherwise, as it would please God to assist and permit them.

In this storme there was a great Venerian shippe of 1100. tun cast away, yet the ship was so set amongst the Rocks, that all her men were saued by the great and mercifull prouidence of almighty God.

Also there were Frenchmen in the Harbor, that cut their Masts ouerboord, and were in great danger, yet all escaped, thankes be giuen to God.

Also afterwards by great good fortune the Exchanges Mast was found by the company betweene two Rocks, and was got on shore, and hauing an excellent good Carpenter, he did workemanlike and strongly scarfe the same with a péce of another Mast, which the Master got from aboord a Flemming, that it brought her well home into England, God be praised.

At our comming to Tripolie wee went to the English house, where wée found one Master Lucas the Vice Consull of Aleppo, and his man, he being factor for the Lading of the Exchange, where wée stayed two daies, and were by him very kindly vsed, and héere we ended our long and tedious Land trauels.

The first day of January being Newyéares day, wee tooke our leaue of Master Lucas, and went aboord, my selfe and Richard Martin, where Captaine Bradshawe also

also vsed vs very kindly, and in regard I was very weake, with long and extreme trauell, he allowed me a good Cabin, and caused the Surgeon to doe mee what good he could.

Tripoly is a Towne of no great traffique, but onely a place whither ships doe come to take in such trading as is brought from other places, and chiefly from Aleppo.

The cause (I thinke) is by reason of the dangerous harbour there. For if there come Easterly windes that ouerblow, there is no safe riding for ships in that harbour. For that no reasonable ground tackle will hold them.

The third day of Ianuary, wee set saile for England, and the one and twentieth day following wee came to the Iland of Zante, where they tooke in three months victuals, which they left there, when they were outward bound.

Also they tooke in Oiles and Currants, being all the Commodities, which the Iland affordes. For of it selfe it is so poore and barren, that it yeeldeth not victuals to maintaine it selfe, but is for the most part maintained from the Maine.

The foure and twentieth day we set saile againe, and about the foure and twentieth day of February the winde tooke vs short, and our Master thinking it not good to beate the ship at Sea with a contrary winde, put into harbour at Malta, where is a gallant harbour, and many gallies and pretty fine shipping belonging to the same, which goe out vpon seruice against the Turke.

Malta is a goodly City of an inuincible strength, with gallant Walls, being built vpon a maine Rocke. And vpon the wals of the olde and new Towne, are peeces of excellent good brasse Ordnance.

And in this City the ansient order of the knights of

K Malta

Malta, haue their continuall residence, who are gallant souldiers, and haue faire houses, not much vnlike to our Innes of Court, they are all Christians, and so are all the inhabitants, viz.

Armenians, Spaniards, Italians, Dutchmen and verie many Frenchmen, the Grand Master of the whole order being a Frenchman, but I could not heare of any English amongst them, yet doe they all shew themselues very kind and courteous to Englishmen.

Also the knights doe weare white and blacke crosses on the shoulders of their cloakes: And any Gentleman that commeth thither, doth put in a stocke of a 100. pound or thereabouts, for his maintenance, but is not allowed for a knight, vntill by seruice against the Turke or elsewhere hee shall deserue the same: and heere wee staied 5. daies.

The 10. day of March, wee set saile againe, and about the 22. day we came to a watch-house where were 2. peeces of Ordnance, and came to an ancor, but because wee came not presently ashore with our boat, they shot at vs, whereupon our Captaine sent our boat on shore with our Boatswaine, who was very kindly vsed, when they knew what wee were, and the Captaine of the watch-house came aboord our ship, & gaue our captaine a liue hog for a present, which hee accepted very thankfully, and requited him with other things of 3. times the value.

And so (as wee thought) hee rested very will contented.

Then our purser and my selfe with a knight of Malta, being a passenger for France, were by our Boatswaine and his gang set on shore, together with the Captaine of the watch-house, wee thinking to goe to the Towne of Callar, to buy such prouision as wee wanted: But the Captaine tooke our Purser and the knight of Malta prisoners, and kept them there: so that our Master not knowing how to come by ye Purser, waigh-

Somewhat is wanting

euanco2 and b2ought the Shippe vp to Callar, and Callar a
went himselfe, and made complaint to the Grand Port-
Seniors, who p2esently granted a discharge fo2 them Towne in
both, and withall p2omised that the Captaine should be Sardinia.
punished fo2 so abusing of his place, and so after foure
daies imp2isonment, the Purser and knight were both
set at liberty and came aboo2d.

Calarie is a great Towne, where a number of Ca- Callari a
uiliers doe liue, and hath some small shipping belong- Towne of
ing to it. Sardinia.

It standeth in the Iland of Sardinia, which is a great
and fruitfull Iland of co2ne and fruit, where wee lay
some fiue daies, and 5. o2 6. daies mo2e off and on, about
the Iland : In which time wee descriued two small
men of warre, which wee imagined to bee some of Captaine Wards crue, who at the first chased vs, and then
we had them in chase, but when they perceiued we were
not fo2 their turne, they made away as fast as they
could, and so we left them.

Then it pleased God to send vs a winde, that b2ought
vs tho2ow the Leuant, and put vs out to the mouth
of the Straits of Gibraltar, from whence wee also The Straits
had a faire winde that carried vs to the height of the of Gibral-
Burlans, which is off the Rocke going to Lisbone in tar.
Portugale, where the winde tooke vs sho2t: So that our
Captaine thought it best to put into Cast Cales, fo2
beating the ship in the sea, which hee did fo2 3. o2 4. daies, Berelen-
vntill it pleased God to send vs a faire winde, and so gas.
putting to sea againe, wee arriued safe in England at the
Towne and po2t of Douer in Kent, about the latter end Douer.
of Aprill, 1611. 1611.

Fo2 which I gaue God thankes, and setting my foot
on English ground, I thought all my miseries to be at
an end.

Fo2 to mée, all the Nations and kingdomes, that in
this my trauels I passed by and saw, both by sea and
land, seemed nothing comparable to it.

R 2 But

But that in respect of them all, it may be called the onely Paradise and blessed Countrey of the world.

And so desiring God of his mercy to blesse every good man from so great miseries as wee indured by the faults and oversight of a lewd and indiscreet Master, being body vnfit and vnworthy to bee imployed in so great affaires, and for so worshipfull and worthy men as were Masters, Owners, and Adventurers therein.

For, Philip de Groue our Master, being a Flemming, an Arch-villaine, who was not onely accused, but it was (by the boy with whom he committed the fact)confessed to my selfe, that hee was a detestable buggerer: So that had not Gods mercy beene the greater, it was a wonder that in regard thereof, and of others being offendors in the like, that our Ship had not suncke in the Ocean.

Lastly, praying to the Almighty, for the long and prosperous raignes of our most Gracious Soueraigne, King IAMES, with the health and prosperity of the Queenes most Excellent Maiesty, and all their Roiall Issue, As also for the Lords of his most Honourable Priuie Councell, and for all the Honourable, Worshipfull, and others, the Masters, Owners and Adventurers, of the Company of the East Indian Merchants, their Factors, Friends, and Wellwillers, I cease, and humbly commit my selfe and this small Relation of my Travels, to their kinde and fauourable Censures.

FINIS.

Printed at Lon-
don, for *Hugh Perry*, in
Brittaines-Burſe.
1631.

CPSIA information can be obtained at www.ICGtesting.com
Printed in the USA
LVOW09s0050121215

466390LV00010B/362/P